The "8" of Us
My Bloodline

The "8" of Us
My Bloodline

Pamela Brown-Dupree

Senior Publisher
Steven Lawrence Hill Sr

BBB
100 YEARS
Advancing Trust Together SM

ASA Publishing Corporation

A Publisher Trademark Title page

ASA Publishing Corporation
An Accredited Publishing House with the BBB
www.asapublishingcorporation.com

The Landmark Building
23 E. Front St., Suite 103, Monroe, Michigan 48161

Copyrights
©2017 Pamela Brown-Dupree, All Rights Reserved
Book Title: The "8" of Us *My Bloodline*
Date Published: 10.16.2017 / Edition 1 *Trade Paperback*
Book ID: ASAPCID2380719
ISBN: 978-1-946746-21-4
Library of Congress Cataloging-in-Publication Data

This book was published in the United States of America
Great State of Michigan

A Publisher Trademark Copyrights page

Table of Contents

Letters

Salutation

Personal Moment

Dedications

The "8" of Us
My Bloodline

Pamela Brown-Dupree

My Childhood
Life with My Mom

Chapter 1

My story begins like this . . .

I can remember being at home with my mother, my stepfather, my five brothers, and two sisters. I think I was about five or six years old and that's when I can remember the child abuse starting. We lived in an apartment in Toledo, Ohio, which had two bedrooms, a living room, a kitchen, a dining room, a back porch, a long hallway, and wooden floors. We even had a balcony.

My first account of child abuse was remembering how my mother treated her children differently from each other. Three of us were treated very badly, while the other five got away with everything. One day, while I was in kindergarten I can remember being a clean little girl, but on this particular day in school I had no underwear on. I don't know if it was because I wet the bed that night, or if it was the fact that we all had different fathers which made it hard for me to adjust to at that age. Never-the-less, I was so embarrassed and the kids teased and made fun of me. When I got home, I could not get in because we were not allowed to come in the front door, and there was a dog in the back of the apartment building, but when I walked down the driveway I would have to peek around the corner of the building to see if the dog was still there.

My mother was very mean. Now don't get me wrong, we did have good times . . . but the bad times stood out the most.

All my other brothers and sisters had to say was that one of us other kids did something wrong and we all got beaten. She had her preference of who got abused more often than the others. Out of the three of us, one of my brothers was given away, but he did come and visit on the weekends. Sometimes during dinner, I was not allowed to sit and eat at the table. She fed me out of a pie tin. I felt like a dog. I remember that mom drank beer all the time. She used to drink Blatt's beer. Even my stepfather drank beer and liquor. Theirs was a violent relationship. He would fight her every weekend. My mom would have had eleven children total but she lost three, probably due to the beating.

One time, one of my brothers accused my second oldest brother and I of drinking her beer, even though he was the guilty one. When he told her that she said, "Since y'all want to drink my beer, I'm going to give you something to drink." She made us drink an old mason jar full of Alaga Syrup and water until we were full. Then she asked us if we were full, and if we wanted some more. My brother said yes, he was full. I said no, and she made me drink another jar full. Sometime during the holidays, we would be watching TV, and I'm not sure what happened, but my mom would tell me to get out. She would try to make me go out in the hallway, but I did not want to. So I told her that I hated her, but that I loved my brothers and sisters. As a result, she made me go into the bedroom and sit by myself all alone.

I always remember being scared. I remember the police being at our house a lot. I remember always being the one in trouble, and most of the time I did nothing wrong. One day my mom and stepdad were fighting and I hid in the closet because I was scared. It was a violent fight as usual. I remember times when two of my brothers would try to protect her after they got older. The violence between my mom and stepdad had us all scared. One thing that I can remember about my mother is that she was a loner. She had only one friend that I can remember and she was a white lady. She went out to the juke joint on the weekend. Sometime my grandmother would come over when my stepdad would start acting up and take us to her house.

Another thing I remember is that my stepdad had another girlfriend and another family. Whenever he and my mom would get into a fight, he would go over to his girlfriend's house and when they fought, he would come back to our house, to our mom. One day, I believe it was back in 1962, my stepdad and mom got into a really bad argument. She had let him come back in the evening. They were in the bedroom arguing really bad. All of us were at home except my brother that was given away. Some of us were in the front room and I was in the other bedroom. All of a sudden, we heard a gun go off, and my mom called my oldest brother, my second oldest brother, and my oldest sister to come and help her because my stepdad had shot her.

They went in the bedroom and saw my mom on the floor, laying in a puddle of blood. They called the police and our grandmother. Before the police got there, my stepdad and his friend picked my mother up from the floor and took her to the hospital. The police showed up afterward and I hid in the closet again because I was afraid. We were all crying. It was then that we were told that my mom was four months pregnant. She lived for a couple weeks after the shooting, but they told us had she lived any longer she would have been a vegetable. You see, she was paralyzed from the neck down. The baby died as well.

My grandmother came and got us and took us to her house to live. That's when my life with my grandmother started. I believe my mom knew she wasn't going to live because everyone was trying to decide who we were going to live with. A decision had to be made as to whether we were all going to stay together, or if we were to be separated. My mother told my oldest sister to tell our grandmother not separate her kids.

Life with
My Grandmother

Chapter 2

After my mother's death, my grandmother legally adopted us, and my brother Tim came back home to live with us for good. I was six years old when we moved in with my grandmother. Later on, we moved to Vance Street and I started attending Gunckel School. I remember being a happy child living with my grandmother. We went to church and my grandmother worked as an insurance lady. I think my grandmother used to be in the military, but I'm not sure. We didn't have much money, even though my grandmother worked. We were also on welfare.

Our house was big inside. We went to school, played with friends, went to church and enjoyed the holidays. I had an aunt and uncle that lived across the street from us. I really don't have any bad memories living at that house. I remembered my first grade teacher, Mrs. Alexander, she would call my grandmother and ask if I could stay at school and have lunch with her. She spoiled me. One day I was at school waiting on my sister to walk home and she didn't show up. So I walked home by myself. I had to walk through an alley to get home. Some little boy started being a bully and tried to fight me, but I ran home crying. I told my brothers about it and after that he didn't mess with me anymore, and I didn't walk home by myself anymore either.

We had after school programs like talent shows. Then came the end of school year, and into the beginning of summer break. When school started the following year, I found out that I got the meanest teacher in school, Mrs. Gray. On the weekends, I used to stay with my aunty and go to church with them. My uncle was a minister and my aunt oversaw Sunday School. She played the piano. I've gone to church as long as I can remember.

I remember one time the Urban Renewal chose my grandmother to help at Christmas time. They brought food, clothes, and toys. They helped us out with whatever we needed or whatever we needed done. Some of us had the chicken pox too. Grandma had to find us a new area to live, because they were getting ready to build an apartment complex. We used to play down the street by Calvary Church, which is still there. One day we saw a man going into convulsions and they had to call the ambulance to come and get him. We had to go home because they wouldn't let us play there anymore that day.

I don't remember when we moved the 2nd time, but we moved farther down Vance Street in the 600 block. We lived in a duplex on the bottom floor. We had three bedrooms, a front room, an office room, and a dining room (we had three ways to get in & out of the house). We had a basement too. I might have been in the 3rd grade going to the 4th grade. All the girls slept in the middle bedroom, grandma slept in the front bedroom and the boys slept in the back bedroom. During this time is when the partying and drinking started, my grandma's friends used to pay us money to dance for them but we couldn't hang around them too long because they were drinking and partying a little too heavy, so we had to either go outside and play, or go in our rooms and play.

I remember my uncle coming over a lot. This went on almost every weekend. Man, we even had chores. We had to make sure the house was clean. Ida had to make sure our hair was combed and that we were cleaned up or else we got in trouble, and so did she. But we couldn't go to the park until my grandmother came home, and that we did everything that we were supposed to do around the house, then we were allowed to leave. We used to go to the park to swim and play on the swings – it was just across the street from where we lived. We used to play with the neighbors and take flashlights and flash them around. That's how we met each other. Their mother was no joke, but she was a sweet person. She used to buy the neighborhood kids ice cream. We played baseball in the park too. We even had one of those old washing machines with the wringer on it, where you turn it with your hands.

My grandmother did a lot of traveling because she was part of the Democratic Party Club. When she would go out of town, she would get a babysitter for us. We had several babysitters. Out of all of them, we only liked two. My cousin, who seemed more like our big brother, and my cousin Sarah, who smoked a pipe. We had a babysitter almost every weekend. My grandmother made sure we went to church every Sunday. If we didn't go to church, then we couldn't go to the movies, or anywhere else for that matter. As we got older, we started walking to church. During Easter time, we would load up in her car and go get our shoes. Sometimes she would trace our foot on brown paper bags and go get our shoes because it was too many of us to go into the store. We would sit down and watch TV until it was time to go to bed.

We always had to eat at a certain time. Grandma would

have a Christmas party after Christmas for all the family. We would listen to music, dance and just have fun. We also had an aunt that we only stayed with on weekends. She was a drinker. She drank Thunderbird Wine and she would dance with us and sing with us. She was very sweet. Her name was Aunt Emma. I also had an aunt named Mary, she partied too. One of our aunt's named Mary used to keep us during spring break to give grandma a break from us kids. As grandma was still going out of town, she started dating this man named Bob. I was around 10 or 11 years old.

Sometimes he would watch us when grandma would leave. He bought us groceries when grandma was home and even when she was out of town. Then he started hanging around and laying in my grandma's bed when she was gone. He only stayed overnight when she was home. He would give us money and the other kids would go to the store but I would stay at home. He would call me to come into the room and tell me not to tell anybody. He would give me money if I let him feel on my breasts. I didn't understand why he did this, but I didn't tell.

My brother would do this to me as well. He would be getting ready to go stay the weekend with my cousin Bruce, who used to babysit us. This is when the incest started. My brother was trying to have sex with me. My grandmother's boyfriend would come over and would go in her bedroom. She would get mad when he didn't come over. He had another girlfriend and she would flatten the tires on my grandma's car. The last time he tried to put his hands on me, I was about twelve. He said we were going to the store to get groceries, instead of going to the store right away, he pulled into the schoolyard, parked the car and tried to have sex with me. It didn't happen because I told him that if he did not stop, I was going to tell on him. I told him to take me home and you know what he did, he paid me to shut up. I never told anyone until I was an adult, and then I only told my psychiatrist.

He took me home and I went outside to play. No one ever knew. Grandma never remarried, she stayed single. You know, thinking back, people used to always give us money. We would go visit the people my mom was that owned the juke joint. These were some of her friends she was around when she was living. We had a play aunt that used to make me clothes, we called her Auntie. We would visit people with grandma and even without her. There was one family that we used to beat up all the time because they acted uppity. I do remember that we had to stay in the yard where grandma could see us, or else we got in trouble. Grandma allowed us to do things after school, like dancing and sports. Roscoe was the only one getting into trouble at school. The parks used to have programs for the kids like swimming contests, beauty pageants which I was in one. I didn't win but that was okay.

One day this lady and her daughter knocked on our door. She was a Jehovah's Witness. She asked my grandma if she had kids and if she had a child her daughter's age to play with. My grandma said yes, Betty. The next time the lady came over to my grandma's, she had her daughter with her. I introduced myself to her. She gave me her name, and then I told her mine. This was actually the first time we've met each other. Soon after, as time has passed, we started playing everyday together with our dolls – we even went swimming together. I was over her house almost everyday, we gotten so close we became sisters. I started even calling her mom, mom.

During this time the little girl had an uncle who would come and visit. He would just look at us playing but never said a word. Then one day when I went over to her house, her aunt and that same uncle were moving in. Later after he settled in, I found out that he was a drinker. He would go outside and sit in her dad's car and get drunk; wasted drunk. On this particular day, we were outside playing and decided to sit on the hood of the car – we were just talking. Then, when I turned around and looked to see what he was doing, he had taken his private out and was trying to get our attention. As kids, we were like, "Auhhh, I'm telling!" We immediately got down off the hood and ran inside and told his wife. She came out so fast and caught him in the act; she got him good, and made that pervert go in the house. This just goes to show you that you can be around other people and stuff like this still goes on.

One day I was at my friend's house, she also had an older brother, but he was seldom home because he works. Someone came and knocked on the door and she went to see who it was. It was her brother's friend. He pretended to look for her brother, but then he asked to use the phone. Instead of him using the phone, he started rubbing his private on me. I got scared and told my friend to get him out. We pretended that we had to leave for something. When he finally left, we ran back in the house and locked the door. This stayed with me for a long time after. I think I was about thirteen. This also started my distrust of men.

Life in the House
on Avondale Street

Chapter 3

Soon, my grandma started looking for a bigger house because we were getting older. And my great uncle was moving in as well, he was blind so he needed help. Well, we finally found a big house on Avondale St. across from Stewart Elementary School, which would be the new school that we would start going to. After we moved, her man friend was still coming around also. I remember I was about eleven years old at the time we moved to Avondale St. This house was huge. It had a dining room, double front room, and a little office off to the side of the dining room. It also had a nice large kitchen. There was a bathroom and pantry off the kitchen. To get to the cellar, you had to go outside. We had a large backyard with a built-in barbecue grill and the backyard was fenced in. We also had flowers.

We had four bedrooms and they were big. We also had a very large attic. My grandmother did some remodeling, including adding a shower in the bathroom. One of my brothers who could draw fixed up the attic and made another bedroom up there. So now we had five bedrooms. The boy's bedrooms were by the attic. When you came up the stairs, straight down the hallway was my grandmother's room. The girls room was off to the left down a little side hallway. I still have the trunk that used to sit in the corner of the hallway. I've had it since I moved where I am now. The next room on the left was my great uncle's room. He was blind and his health was not very good. The problems of arguing and fights still didn't start till a few years after we settled in. My grandmother still had her picks. The only time things were good was around the holidays. We always ate dinner as a family, usually around 6PM. Our cousins used to stay with us on the weekends and my uncle Dale stayed with us as well. He was divorced from his first wife but his two kids he had with her stayed with us on weekends. I used to love to comb and braid my little cousin's hair. I used to babysit them and I got paid.

We played outside all the time. We played baseball, volleyball, kickball, and hopscotch. We lived across the street from the school, so we played on the playground. In the summer, when it was real hot, somebody would hook up a hose to the fire hydrant and put it through the fence at the school and we would get wet. At least we weren't worried about getting ran over. My grandmother worked during the day for some rich white people. She would clean their house and babysit their kids. During Christmas time, my grandmother's employers would give us a Christmas tree. Their daughter's names were Meg and Wendy. My grandmother also did taxes every tax season out of her home. We still had to be in front of the house at 6PM or we got into trouble.

Then my grandmother got a job with the government, working for the Urban Renewal Program. She had to get a sitter, which was my oldest sister to watch us while she was at work. It didn't last long because we were getting older. She was still getting assistance to help take care of us. When we were younger, my grandmother did a lot of traveling to Cleveland and Washington, D.C. She met John F. Kennedy, who was President of the United States at the time. She was also a member of the Democratic National Party. She used to hold meetings and parties at our house. When she would go out of town, my oldest brother would throw house parties. She didn't even know until she came home. Those parties got wild and then fights started and the police would come. My neighbors would call because it was loud, cars parked in front of their houses, and fights outside. I got scared, and because I don't like the police. Whenever she would go out of town, I would be like "oh boy" I don't like this. We were still a family. We'd watch TV together, but we had to be quiet or else we had to go to bed, and we had better say our prayers before we go to bed.

After church on Sunday, we would go home, eat dinner and then grandma would take us to Dairy Queen for ice cream. We would go to our auntie's house in Toledo, Ohio for a few hours. We also had an aunt that lived in Detroit, she was my grandmother's sister. And, during spring break we would go stay a week with her. It was fun going there. They would party and drink. My grandmother would have birthday parties for us. Around Christmas time, we would help cook all the food. My grandmother would hide our gifts until we went to bed. She did this to make us think we weren't going to get anything. Every year on New Year's Day, my grandmother would have a family get-together. Only the grown-ups could drink the eggnog because grandma would put liquor in it. Wherever we moved, my Aunt Emma would always make sure she came where we were. She would come over to talk and play with us. She was a drinker. When it was time for bed, she would make sure we had our baths and said our prayers before we went to sleep. I was going on 13 then.

Grandma still had her job at the Urban Renewal. We had to do chores and they had to be done by the time she got home or we would get in trouble. If they were done when she came home, we were able to go outside. I remember being about 13 or 14 when my oldest brother Robert went into the Navy. We had a party for him before he left. My uncle still lived with us. When he got off work, I used to like going shopping with him. He would take us all riding in his Thunderbird, which was white, and he would make his car jump up and down and it was fun. He used to scare us, and when we got in trouble, he would make us put a book on our heads and stand in the corner with one leg up. We had many after school programs. One was running track. As we got older, our grandmother decided that we didn't a sitter anymore, but her friend would check on us. She would leave us money for milk, cereal and bread.

Then we started meeting the neighbors around us on Avondale. We would play with their kids. Next door to us lived the Jones. We ended up calling them grandma and grandpa, their kids were grown. On Fridays, my grandma would let us go to Teen Town, but not at first because we would argue and they would get mad at me because I wouldn't help my other two sisters clean up our bedroom. My grandmother bought our house from an old spooky looking white man. The reason I'm telling you this, is because we had some really large closets, and we hung long curtains in front of it because it always felt like someone was watching us. We still had fights and arguments. I believe that it all trickled down to the girls because it was just the boys fighting at first. My grandmother would let my older brother chastise the younger brothers. He thought he could do anything and he thought he was in control of us. We hated it. If we were on the phone, he always had to use it. She would not even try to stop the fight.

You know my grandmother would never change her clothes in her bedroom. She would change them in the dining room and my baby brother picked up the same disgusting habit. She didn't even teach us about personal hygiene. It was my sister Ida and my Aunt Emma. When I was thirteen, I got to go to summer camp, Local 112. My other aunt started talking about us and our clothes, and then I did not want to go to her house anymore. She was mean. The next time she came to get us, I would not go because she said nasty things about us and put us down. She acted like we weren't good enough. She even said I didn't want to come because I was thinking about boys. Another reason I did not want to go is because one night she went looking for her boyfriend in the bar and she left me and my youngest sister in the car by ourselves for a long time, and we were scared. She said not to open the door for anyone, so we got down on the floor of the car. One time while I was still in Junior High School, my girlfriend Michelle and I went to the YMCA to play pool. When we left the YMCA, a guy in a car pulled up and started talking to us. He was actually flirting with me.

I was getting ready to start High School, and was about 16 yrs. old, and I met this boy named Danny after my Sweet 16th Birthday Party. Once I met him, you couldn't tell me anything. I started sneaking out to meet and talk to him. We weren't having sex yet. I started hanging out at the bar with my sister Ida and this was the first time I got drunk (drinking Strawberry Hill). I was going to Libbey High School at the time.

You couldn't tell me anything about Danny. One day, my grandmother came home and she was looking for me. My baby sister told my grandmother that I had went to meet Danny. My grandmother came looking for me. Diane showed grandma where I was. She told him that I was only a minor and he could go to jail. Grandma threatened to send me to CSB *Children Services Bureau*. I was very rebellious after that and I hated my sister. I was always saying I was going to run away. I thought I was in love with Danny, but it was puppy love.

My friend started getting scared because I told her that sometimes I could feel someone pulling my hair. One day we skipped school at my house and my friend Michelle said it felt like someone was pulling her hair too. She got scared, so we went out of the house to make it look like we had just came home, and she fell off the porch. She said somebody pushed her off.

After that, she never would come back over. I would have to go over her house. I always thought that that was my mother. I always felt her presence, even though I didn't like her. My grandmother had this little man friend that would come over on the weekends and we couldn't have company because she did not want them to see her with him. This set a habitual pattern with men for us girls. She had one boyfriend in Cleveland. Now Mr. Bob was dating another woman and grandma got upset because she could not find him or he wouldn't come over. She would make us tell our company they had to leave. One time when my auntie from Detroit came to visit, my grandma took my aunt with her to find Mr. Bob. When she found him, she snatched him up and started fighting him because he hadn't come over or called her.

Mr. Bob finally got tired of my grandmother stalking him, so he called the house and my brother answered the phone. Mr. Bob told him he was going to mess up grandma, and he hung up. Then he called back again and I answered the phone and he said, "I'm tired of your grandma looking for me. When I hide my car, she finds it. She's at my house. I'm tired and I'm just going to stop messing with her." I told my Uncle

Dale and he said, "He better not mess with my momma!" I then told my uncle what Mr. Bob said on the phone. Mr. Bob stopped messing with my grandma.

During this time is when I had my first child, Jewel, my grandmother was upset with me. She was going to kick me out. My sister knew I was pregnant because she took me to the clinic. I think I got pregnant just to get away from my grandmother. I was 17 at the time. My granny told me to keep the baby and she was going to send me to the Florence Crittenton School. I told her I wasn't going to give my baby away. She gave my sister permission to take me to the doctor. She told me not to call her when I went into labor, and that I better call that boy Danny. After Mr. Bob left her alone, my grandmother ended up having a nervous breakdown.

What on Earth Could Go Wrong, Now?!

Chapter 4

Now for the crazy stuff . . .

My grandma was still going by his house after he left her alone. She went to the doctor and he gave her some pills, but she didn't get better and ended up in the hospital. She was in the hospital about a week. Her daughter came to see her, and so did my uncle Bill. My great uncle and aunt came to see her after she got out of the hospital. She was so sick that she couldn't be by herself. She met this lady that lived on our block and one that lived on Belmont. They started praying for her, one would pray and then the other one would pray for her.

Grandma still didn't get any better. In fact, she may have gotten worse, because she thought somebody or one of the two ladies put a voodoo spell on her. I was the one that was home with her, so I saw everything that went on. One day my aunt and uncle came over and I had a chance to leave the house. Oh, by the way, my oldest brother got to see how she was acting. Our neighbor down the street brought this man over to pray for grandma. They were upstairs and she had no clothes on except her girdle and my brother made the comment, "What they got to do, soup her up first, they full of crap." He left me there alone. She started going through the house humming and rubbing her hands and talking about me, and said, "I know she smoking that stuff." I told her to leave me alone and I put my baby's coat on and left.

I went to my girlfriend's house to get my hair done and my cousin came looking for me and told me to come back home until somebody can get here to be with her. When I finally decided to go home, everybody else was already there. I told them that there was nothing wrong with her except that Mr. Bob scared her. He told her that he would beat her up if she didn't leave him alone. He left her alone and she started getting better.

My grandmother wouldn't give me money for my baby, even though I knew she had it. She kept saying she didn't have any left. But you know, I made my way. I found a cleaning job with one of my friends and her mother. That's when I told them to take me off of welfare because she wasn't giving it to me anyway. Plus, my brother called and said to take him off too. My grandmother was even trying to turn my brother against me. We were always close. Then he moved to Atlanta. He was upset with me before he left because grandma had turned him against me. Something happened to him after he moved to Atlanta. He found a job making good money. He called me and wrote me. He told me he would send me money and he did through the mail. I told him not to come back here to Toledo because he was doing really well for himself. I was still working with my best friend's mom and I had a little money coming in too. I would do anything to stay away from my grandma's house. My brother Roscoe came home from Atlanta and started dating this lady named Neat. They got married and she had a baby.

I found two friends to help me with my child for daycare and their names were Momma Joe and Momma Mary from down south. We really got close. My son was between 4 and 9 months old. My grandma was still trying to control what time I came in. They lived on Ewing in an apartment building. Everybody just hung out around there. Then I would leave at night with Danny and go to his sister's house. You couldn't tell me anything about Danny. I was hardheaded when it came to him. I was young and head over heels in love with him until I started to see how he really mean he was, being on drugs and having a lot of other women. You know, even if my baby was sick, I would still have my baby with me. They tried to tell me but I wouldn't listen, until I got fed up with him. Then one day I was at Momma Mary and Momma Joe's house and I was getting ready to walk home and there was a blue GTO convertible parked and the guy inside had been watching me.

As I started walking down the street, somebody called my name, it was Danny. He had been following me. He followed me all the way to Avondale and told me to get in the car, and I told him NO! He wanted to argue about another man touching his baby. I may have talked to him a little while longer, but I eventually left him alone for good (he was abusive also). I had to find out for myself that he was no good. What made me leave him alone is that he called me to bring him something to his sister's house, and I found him in the room with another woman. I was a little stupid because he would say really sweet things to me to make me change my mind about him. We were still talking when his sister moved over on Smead.

The last straw was when he was using some strange drug and he flipped out on me. One day I went to his sister's house and he was on the phone with another woman and I picked up the phone and he was so angry with me. I was going to call my sister-in-law to pick me up. He was so mad that he said, "Ain't nobody going to sleep," and he picked up his son and shook him to wake him up out of his sleep. My sister-in-law picked us up and took us home. I left him alone after this. He would try to act crazy and intimidate me. He didn't really do anything for his son and after I left him, he really didn't do anything after that.

Then I started hanging out, going to the bars and stuff in the neighborhood. Then I met this guy named Jerry. He was a real nice guy, but he was a drinker (he drank Wild Irish Rose). My son was about 8 or 9 months old at the time. He had a red Cadillac called the "Red Goose". We were just talking because he was already dating someone. We did different things like going to the drive-in. We would just sit around Momma Joe and Momma Mary all day and chill. One day in the summer of '73 or '74, Jewel touched the window and it fell on his hand and when we raised the window, blood was gushing out. Bobby slammed down the hood of his car and took Jewel and I to St. V's hospital. The nurses took him from me and my shirt was full of blood. They stitched up his finger from the front to the back. They really took care of him. They told me to change his bandage, don't touch the wound and give him medicine if he needed it. Now I'm dating Jerry and he met grandma and she liked him. There was nothing he would not do for her. Then my grandma started up more lies again telling my sisters and brothers that I was not changing my son's bandages and not feeding him. That was a lie. I made a deal with Jerry, I told him that I would go with him if he quit drinking and he said, "You will?" and I said "Yea." He said for me to think about it for a couple of days and the next time I saw him, he had quit drinking and we started dating.

We did fun things together. He started working with

MC Sutton at a restaurant. He went in at night and would get off at 4 or 5 in the morning. I started going with him to the restaurant. I took my son with me (while they worked, I watched). Grandma started saying that I was not cleaning my child up and not coming home at night. She just wanted me to come back home, but I didn't want to. I was grown. I kept spending the night with Jerry but eventually I went back home. Grandma didn't mind Jerry staying over for little while at night. He would leave about 11:00PM, but she would complain about the lights and TV being on. Her little boyfriend was still coming around. One time he got so high that he went to sleep and I couldn't get him to wake up. I asked grandma if he could stay the night and she said yes, but I couldn't sleep next to him.

The funniest thing happened, because after he slept off his high, he was getting ready to leave and his other girlfriend pulled up next to his car and they got to fighting, down on the corner from our house. He finally left and she did too. He started backing off a little. We started back dating again after a while. During that time Grandma had met a younger guy named Sam. He was ok, but grandma did her own thing. I knew she was sleeping with him because they would go upstairs to her room. One time we were sitting and watching TV and she got mad at Jerry. I guess because she had left that boy alone. One day we saw him go right up in the house and went right up to her room. Jerry went to get him and make him leave. Grandma started being nice to Jerry again because he looked out for her.

Jerry started drinking again. Then my cousin Phyllis moved in. She and Jerry were cool and we all got along together. She knew Jerry's ex-wife. She would see his ex out in a club or somewhere and tell her, "My cousin is dating your man and you bet not mess with her." That started problems and Jerry heard about it. Then he and my cousin fell out about it, they got into an argument and my cousin told lies to my grandma about Jerry and she made him leave again. So now we would talk outside in his car. My cousin started causing problems with everybody in the house. Grandma seemed to like her because she was taking sides.

Me and Jerry would get together on weekends and spend them at a motel, while my girlfriend would watch my son for me. Soon stuff came up missing and no one knew who took it. One day I came in from the doctor, and my cousin was chasing after my baby sister trying to fight her. My sister was pregnant. Jerry's friends were asking him if I was pregnant because I looked like it. I called the doctor to find out for sure if I was and he said I was.

My brother Tim was defending my sister, and was in the front room. I got so fed up that I was going to get her. She ended up leaving. I went to the store and plus I was looking for him to tell him that I was pregnant. He had already asked me if I had something to tell him. When I told him that I was pregnant, he was so happy. We got back together. I was going into my 2nd month. Grandma gave us the house and she moved to Palmwood Ave. It seemed that everybody who didn't have a place to live, she would send them to us on Avondale because she wasn't letting them move in with her. They could live rent free because me and my sister Ida was paying the rent and everything else except the water bill, grandma paid that bill.

My cousin started doing crazy stuff like jumping out of cabs and not paying, so they wouldn't even come to our house anymore (by now I had two children and my sister had 1). Grandma sent my cousin back to stay with us again. Things were okay at first but then stuff started to get stolen from me and Diane. At first, we didn't know if it was her, so we set her up. We put some food stamps in one of our dresser drawers in the bedroom. It was a $65 book. She took it because she was rambling. What took the cake this time was she had jumped out of the cab with a man and they both were high, and I told her that she was not coming up with that man around our kids. So she got mad and started cussing. She was coming upstairs to fight us because she had that man with her. I had my brother's BB gun and turned it around backwards to clobber her with it.

I was standing on my bed and my baby sister had the banister drew back to whoop her. She was mad and stole more food stamps from me. She also said that we weren't going to have anyone in the house either and I told her, "You don't pay no rent and no bills." I called grandma and let her know what was going on and told her that she better not come back over or else we were going to kill her dead. She never came back for a long time (it took years). My cousin came back with one of our old neighbors. She apologized to us. She told the old man that we were mean and didn't take mess off of anyone. We just talked for a while and then she left. Things got a little better. My other sister moved in with us, so now it was all of us together with our kids living in the same house. We shared the bills. Ida was the organizer of the family and she helped us out. Things were okay for a while. We would have our little parties and holidays together. Everyone got along. Then chaos broke out again. Me and Ida would take turns watching each other's kids. Diane didn't see eye to eye with us and she would take off and leave her kids without asking. So we would call grandma and tell on her. Then Diane moved her little man friend in our house and then there were a whole lot of problems.

Me and Ida would call grandma and tell her to come and get Diane's kids because we weren't going to watch them. My grandma ran to Diane's rescue a lot. We told grandma that we were going to find somewhere to live on our own. Ida moved out first, Diane moved out next, and left me there with the high water bills and no one offered me any help with them. My lights got turned off (I had a job at the time). Someone turned the lights back on, but they did it illegally. In order to get them back on the right way, we had to pay the bill plus a deposit, which was about $500. Things went back to normal for a little while. It was just my two children and I, and my brother Roscoe. Finally, I made up my mind to move, and I found a place. Roscoe ended up staying in grandma's house by himself and I went on to the next stage of my life. Before I get to my life's story, let me give you a little background history on my brothers and sisters, starting with Roscoe.

Roscoe was the hell raiser of the family, and he was mean. He wasn't like this at first, but time and circumstances changed his attitude, his behavior and his life. He did things that he was not happy about. It upset him very much and it took a toll on his demeanor. He used to have to get a good and bad card to get in school. Back then, in order to get back in school they gave him a good and bad report card, because he used to kick teachers down the stairs and this was in grade school. As kids, he would trick people into doing things. One time my mom gave him a party and there was this fat girl that wanted to dance with him and he didn't want to dance with her, so she chased him. My brother was also a fire bug, he used to set bugs on fire and he set our apartment on fire as well. He may have been mad at our mother and he didn't care. He went to Gunckel School with us. He was in a talent show at school because he could sing really well. Then he went on to High School and we saw an even bigger change in him. I don't remember him playing any sports, but the girls liked him. He used to have two friends where he would go and spend the night and they came over to our house as well. He finally graduated high school.

Most of his friends were taller than him and they played basketball. He started hanging out, partying, drinking and doing drugs. He used to sing in two different groups on stage. They could sing so well that they tore the place up. He had a couple of different jobs. He bought his first car when he was older. I don't remember how old he was though. He was an excellent swimmer and he was on the swim team at City Park. He could run fast, and was on the track team as well. As he got older, you could see more changes beginning to take place in him.

He would travel a little with his friends and then he got married. I don't remember what year though. He had two children (only one was with his wife). I don't remember how long he was married. He and his wife went through a lot. He began to be physically abusive toward her and no one knew why. Eventually she got tired and kicked him out. They did not divorce right away, but they did a while later down the road. He always used profanity, especially when he was drinking and fighting. After they separated, he moved in with our sister Ida. I do have to say this about my brother, he had a good heart. He was very over-protective of us girls.

He would not let anyone hurt us. He never remarried, but he had plenty of girlfriends. The abuse continued in each of his other relationships. The drinking, drugs, partying, and gambling continued. Even when he was hanging out, he would get into fights. After a while, he moved back to Avondale St. You know, he always had really good jobs when he was working. He was really good at fixing up houses like a handyman or a carpenter, and he enjoyed it.

As he got older, you could still see the negative changes happening to him. It started to show in almost everything he did, and I know why. He would always deny it and say, "Ain't nothing wrong with me." He wouldn't let go of the past, his past. He would always say that he didn't need any professional help. Even today, his past still haunts him because he won't let it go. I have to tell you that when he started hanging out, I would hang out with him as I got older to keep him out of so much trouble. To end this about my brother, he would look out for me and no one could mess with me, and I could look out for him, too. I do love my brother Roscoe with his crazy self! Ha, ha, ha!!!

Now let me tell you about my sister Ida. She was the little momma of the family. She just thought she had to take care of us. I don't really remember everything about Ida when we were all living with my mother as far as what had to do with us, but I can tell you about our life after our grandmother took us in. Ida had to make sure us girls were clean and had our hair combed. We were little girls and she may have been around the age of 12 maybe. She had to make sure the house was clean before Grandma came home from work. When she would comb my hair, she would put these two little skinny braids on either side of my head and we would always argue about it because I didn't like it. As Ida got older, she got pregnant when she was 14 or 15. Her first child was a girl and my grandmother wanted her to get married and she didn't want to. She did pretty good in school even with a baby.

She eventually went to high school so she could graduate. She went to Libbey High School. Ida was a bookworm and wanted a better life when she grew up than what she had as a kid. She went to night school and she did graduate. She also worked different jobs. She used to work for the Unemployment Office, and when they would close for the summer, she had to get welfare (she did not like this at all), but she would always look for a better job. She worked for the school and she worked for Goodyear. Ida used to watch me and when I got older, we would argue and get into fights. When I had my first child, she bought him all kinds of clothes and things. She helped me out a lot with him, but I always thought she hated me.

She was still being our little momma because Grandma was always traveling. She made sure we ate and everything. When I turned 16, she gave me a Sweet 16 party. Months later I started trying to hang out with her. She would let me, but she wouldn't let me drink because I was not old enough yet. I would sneak my drinks any way. One night she went out and she went looking for her boyfriend Ben. She thought he was in the bar but he wasn't. Somebody in the bar told her that they knew where he was and the guy who told her about her boyfriend drugged her and something bad happened to her when she went to find him. After this, she went through some problems behind it. One day after being tired of being laid off and getting welfare, she landed a really good job with the State of Ohio as a clerk. She then bought her first house.

Ida used to party on the weekends, but she did take care of her kids. One day she got married and things changed for the better, so we thought. They were married in his mom's house. He was older than her. We did not know that he was a violent person. When we found out, we also knew that she fought him back, and Roscoe came to the rescue. Her husband would mess with her so much that we would have her come and stay with us a little while. Sometimes I would go and stay with her because her husband would call and threaten her. One day I called her and told her that I would come and stay with her. He just kept calling and he threatened her and told her he was going to burn the house down with her and the kids in it. He didn't know he was talking to me. Finally, I got so fed up that I cussed him out and told him to come on over, and that the door was open. He came and I cussed him out again and he finally left her alone and then they eventually separated after that.

Ida had a birthday coming up, so we decided to give her a surprise party because she had been through so much. I invited some of everybody to her party, even some of her old boyfriends and even her husband. I remember telling Ida about my dream that I opened the door and her husband came in and I chopped his head off. A few years later, Ida moved out of her house and moved back to Avondale, where me, her and the kids lived together for a while. We ended up getting closer as we got older. Then things changed again. She had a nervous breakdown. I was very worried about my sister. I would go to the hospital with her. Sometimes we thought she was doing well, but deep down inside she was not okay.

She still did things like go to Bingo because she liked that, but everything was not okay. I would watch the kids for her. Eventually Ida got better. She still had her job as a clerk with the State of Ohio. Then an opportunity for a better position with the State came along. She took the job making better money and she moved to Columbus with her children. Grandma let Ida take her little white car to Columbus, it lasted for a while. She had to find her another place to live. She still works for the State and she still lives in Columbus with her children and grandchildren.

Going Through the Mill
with My Brothers

Chapter 5

My brother Tim is the fifth oldest child. Tim was a cute little boy with pretty eyes. As a kid I don't think he had a good life because he was separated from us by our mother. She gave him to our stepfather's sister. I don't know if she really wanted him. I'm just not sure what that was all about. We would see him on the weekends when he would come over. I can't really remember a whole lot about Tim as a kid or even playing with him outside. When grandma took us in, Tim was not an 'A' student in school and Grandma would constantly put him down. Tim went to an all-boys school and so did Roscoe. Tim was a helpful person and he always had a job. Coming up as kids, we would fight with each other. We used to play grocery store. Tim liked to play tricks on us, too. We would sit around together and watch TV. One time while we were eating dinner, he ate something and grandma made him eat a whole pot of potatoes for no reason, and little momma Ida spoke up for him and she got in trouble too. Tim ended up having three children, one girl and two boys (different mothers). He always stayed into arguments with his girlfriends and he could not drink at all.

When he did, he would bring up certain things about our mother and he would cry a lot and Roscoe would pick on him.

The mothers of his kids would all dog him a lot and he was not around his kids a lot when they were little. Tim worked for Bobby in a store. We used to tease him and say that Bobby was his other daddy because Bobby would do a lot for Tim and keep him on his toes. One of his kid's momma introduced him to drugs and we didn't know for a long time. She belittled him all the time as a man. I would talk to him about getting professional help but he would refuse to do it. Tim just really wanted someone to love him. He never got that love from momma or grandma. That's why he didn't know how to treat his own kids or women. He bought himself a car and he was doing ok for a while.

He would hang out with us every now and then. As Tim got older, he started messing with cocaine and hanging around the wrong people. I tried to talk to him about getting help. He still refused. The drugs made everybody not want to be around him. Tim's daddy was an alcoholic as well and he was violent too. One day when I lived on Woodland, I called him up and asked him to come and help me move something. While he was there, we had some beer and I told him to get some help. I told him not to do it for me, but to do it for himself. Maybe a week after we talked, he went into a rehab program for 60 or 90 days.

He also needed surgery to remove a hernia that he had. I let him come and stay a couple of days to recuperate, but as soon as he was healed and better, he went back around the wrong people and got involved with drugs again. He still had his job though. Sometimes it would be weeks before I would see him or talk to him. I do believe my bother Tim spoke to a counselor while he was in rehab. I think maybe my brother had too many demons. The last time he got out, Grandma called and said she was worried because he had nowhere to go, and no one knew where he was. She said someone had come to her house and planted flowers but she didn't know who did it. We found out that it was Tim who planted the flowers. My brother did not want me to see him like he was, back on the drugs again. Then along came a new drug called 'ice'. It took a toll on him and he just lost control of who he was. The drugs had total control of him. He went to grandma's house and she put him down, calling him stupid and other negative stuff. Because of this, the worst tragedy of all happened.

Tim and grandma had words and he picked up an iron and hit her with it several times in the head. She tried to fight back, but he was stronger than she was. It was on a Saturday morning that her son found her dead and he called the police. We knew that it was somebody she must have known because she had a bat in the corner of her bedroom, and she never picked it up to defend herself. I really do believe in my heart that my brother just lost his mind. The way they found out that Tim did it was because we started calling all the family and no one could find Tim. He eventually turned himself in. He is doing 25 to life and 5 to 25 in prison now as this is being written.

Bobby is the baby. I remember Bobby was two months old when our mother died. Bobby has two birth defects. Bobby always thought that Ida was his mother because she had to take care of him after our mother died. As he grew up, he was a little kiddified. He used to rock back and forth a lot and whine when he was little. He liked model cars. As he got older and started going to school, he was a cry baby and he didn't do well in there. He would get lost coming home and we just lived around the corner. I would always have to go and pick him up. Bobby was in special classes because he was a little slow.

He did graduate from school. I don't remember Bobby

ever having a job, but he did have a girlfriend named Kelly. Bobby was heartbroken when he and Kelly broke up. When Bobby turned 18, I heard that my sister Diane or Roscoe turned him onto drinking and marijuana. I'm not sure which one of them did. He did not handle it well at all. It made him act strange. His nieces and nephews did not like being around him because he would tickle and touch them and they did not like it. He was on medication too. Grandma would have to pick him up from school because he would have a bad day. The kids were scared of him. He would end up in the state hospital because of the drugs and his medication. We had a cousin that moved in with us and she had two boys. She caught Bobby messing with them and threatened to kill him. She told grandma but grandma did not do anything about it.

One day he met a girl named Mary and they got married. I think she knew something was wrong with my brother. She was the kind of person that misused handicapped people. They had their 1st anniversary at my grandma's house and I threatened her. I told her that if she misused my brother she was going to have to answer to me. Bobby had a best friend named Fred. Bobby, Fred, Mary, and Hazel hung around together. Mary started mistreating my brother. She started telling him she was pregnant, but I knew he couldn't have babies because of his medication. I didn't care for Mary because I knew she was using my brother. One particular day I remember he went into the hospital and Mary was messing around with another man. Me and Tim went to their house and I threatened her again and Tim told me to behave myself. Where they lived, they had drug dealers over them. Mary left my brother at the hospital and grandma had to go get him. Some kind of way Mary got him back home. I called grandma and she said Bobby was at home at his house. I was upset, very upset.

You see, Bobby was on a fixed income. When he had no money, Mary was not around. When it came time for him to get his money, she would come back around. She called grandma and asked if her and Bobby could come and stay because something fell out of their ceiling. I told Grandma to let Bobby come and stay, but to let Mary stay where she was. Mary would tell my brother that she was having twins, so he started telling everybody else. The next day was check day and I called and asked where Bobby was. My cousin said that Mary came and got him. I called Diane to come and get me and we went to Grandma's house and asked our cousin where they went. She said probably around the corner to Fred's house. So we went over to Fred's house and knocked on the door. I asked Fred where Bobby was and he said he was in there. I kind of pushed him out of the way and went in. Bobby was talking to Grandma on the phone trying to get her to let Mary move in. I told her she better not or I'm going to chase her out of there. It was not anything nice because I reminded her about mistreating my brother.

I was getting ready to hit her because she told my brother that she had a miscarriage. I told her she was a liar, and she was not even pregnant. I don't know what she was doing with him, but she was buying him porno movies. That was how she tried to keep him around her. Lying about being pregnant. The last time he went into the hospital, he moved back with Grandma. She tried to get him but it didn't happen.

Diane was the baby girl. She was spoiled. She liked having her way, and she was a scaredy cat. She was also scared of midgets. When she would act bad or tell on us, we would tell her, "Little man gonna get you," and she would run and tell Grandma. As she started getting older and going to school, I remembered how beautiful she used to sing. She wanted to hang around me, but I didn't want her to because she was a tattle tale. She liked to dress up. One time she went downtown with her little friends and they would steal. She kept stealing until one day we got a phone call that the police was holding her at the store for stealing, and we had to go get her. Diane is also the glamour girl, she likes to dress and have money, lots of it.

She also likes to party. I believe that Diane had a jealous streak in her too. She always kept a job, and she would get people in trouble. One job she had, she worked in a bar. We would go hang out and party with her. Then she started dating different men. Some were good relationships, some were bad. Diane had two kids around about this time. She always wanted to be right, and as we got older, we didn't get along that well because I didn't do the things she did. She had her own friends and I had my own. Yes, Diane did a lot of partying. In some of the relationships she had, the men would fight her and that reminded me of my mom. She wouldn't defend herself, she was scared. Sometimes I would defend her and tell them that they are not going to hit her. Her and Ida hung out together more than her and I did. They thought I was sneaky.

I really didn't like hanging with her because I had my own circle of friends and she would always tell on me. As she got older, she met another guy and he seemed nice. He had a nice job and they had a nice home together. Diane was also into taking pills. She might have stopped when she met Barry, I'm not sure, but twins came out of this relationship. She was insecure about the relationship because he was a big flirt. He looked good and he knew it. I really do believe he was trying to make her jealous by the way he was acting. Diane thought that we always gave her a hard time.

When we were younger, Robert would protect us. He would not let anyone mess with us. He used to throw wild parties when Grandma went out of town. The neighbors would call the police and that was the only way Grandma found out about the parties. He paid us not to tell.

You see, my brother Robert was the pretty boy. Nice hair, good looking, dressed nice, and everybody liked him. He had a flock of women and he partied hard when he did party. His hang out was on Dorr Street. Sometimes he would date two women at one time. Then he started having kids. As of this date, he only has four kids. He never married even though he told them they were going to get married. He ended up going into the Navy. I don't remember how long he was there, but he came out with an honorable discharge. He got into a fight with a guy in the Navy about a girl and got stabbed.

When he came home from the military, he was very bossy, always telling us what to do. He and Roscoe did not get along. They stayed into it a lot. He always kept a nice car. I don't remember if he went back to school or not or even if he graduated. Robert did not get along with his dad but he did go around him, especially in the bar. As we got older, Robert didn't really hang around us that much anymore. He moved out and got his own place. We only saw him if we were having something special. He still parties right now to this very day.

However he did raised one of his kids. Losing grandma took a lot out of him. He had a really good job. Later he ended up on disability. He was not the big brother he should have been because he was not there when we really needed to talk to him. I love him, but he missed out on a lot with us because he wasn't there. Our birthdays are close together, mine is June 24th and his is June 25th. He used to come to my house on holidays because he liked my food, my good cooking.

I have been saved 12 years. Since then he has come to my house a few times. The last time he came to my house, he was high. He got upset because I didn't have any liquor in the house. That's when I gave my life to the Lord. Then he stopped coming around. I think maybe he has slowed down a little from the partying. He lives by himself and I think he is doing okay. I must say this, my brother ended up on medication for depression, just like the rest of us. Generational curse.

Sherman is the smart one, the brains of the bunch. I can remember him at 5 years old. He was sick. My brother's face got burned on a radiator because he's a rocker. He bumped into it or something. One time the doctor came to our house and gave him a shot and he yelled out loud. The doctor gave me a shot in my booty. He wasn't scary, he was just quiet. As we got older, we started calling him the Nutty Professor. He was always around us so we played a lot. We went swimming, riding bikes, things like that.

He graduated from high school. He and Tim hung around each other until they went their separate ways. He loved to draw, he was a good artist. He did a little partying, not a lot. Sometimes we would party and he would be watching TV. He went to the Navy a little while after he graduated. I believe he didn't like the surroundings and that's why he joined. We gave him a going away party before he left. It was a big party with lots of food. Our favorite Aunt Emma was there. He stayed in the Navy a long time.

I remember when he was in the Navy, he sent for me to come to Charleston, SC to visit but I had to fly. I was afraid of flying because my oldest son dreamed that the plane crashed. So I rode the bus for 22 hours to get there. We stayed at one of his Navy friends' house, Pete and Sharon. He showed me a really good time. We went to a picnic. Most of his Navy friends were white. We went bowling and I won a trophy for being the goofiest on the team. I don't remember him drinking a lot or doing drugs. He may have smoked a little marijuana, but beer was his thing. Whenever he would come home on leave, he would hang out with a group of his friends and they would party at somebody's house.

During his visits, he would play with his nieces and nephews. They would play games like Monopoly, Pictionary, and stuff like that. We didn't have the same father. While he was in the Navy, he ended up getting married but he didn't stay married long. He ended up getting a divorce. He had two sons. I saw certain changes take place as he got older. I didn't understand what had happened to him while he was in the Navy. He and his wife got along. They lived with my grandmother after he got out for a little while, and then he went back down south. Somehow he took the boys away from their mother and he raised them.

For a while, I did not hear from him. He was doing things he should not have been doing. I think he went back into the service but not for long. He asked if my oldest son could come and help him with the boys. I let him go and he mistreated my son. My dad told him that he would put the law on him. Let me tell you, I didn't really know if he liked men or women. I didn't know! Sometimes we wouldn't hear from him for years. I guess he was just doing his own thing. Now his kids are grown and he is living in Los Angeles, CA and working. I guess he's doing ok.

Let me back up to Danny and I, and how he was, and how many children he had besides my son Jewel. I met Danny while walking down the street. I was 17 at the time. I was with my friend Michelle and we were coming from the YMCA. This man pulled up next to us in a sporty car. He asked both of us our names and we told him. He said he wanted to talk to me. As I said before, I lived on Avondale and he lived around the corner on Belmont. I would sneak around to see him and I knew he was older than me. He stayed with his cousin. I continued to sneak and see him until my baby sister Diane found out and snitched on me to Grandma.

He ended up moving with his sister on Pinewood down by Third Baptist Church. Listening to the sweet talk that he was throwing down to me made me think I knew everything. He was a handsome looking man, but I didn't know how many women he had. Now my family knew that I was talking to him, and they didn't like it at all. Then he started hanging around my brother Tim, and our cousin Ricky. I was sneaking in the bar even though I wasn't old enough. They let me in because I acted older than my age. Finally, I started seeing some of Danny's hidden secrets.

I used to meet him down at the corner when he called and said he was coming. I introduced my adopted sister Teresa to Danny because I knew she wouldn't tell on me. He picked us up and we would go riding and I didn't drink a lot, just a little. Then one day we were in the car together and Danny was acting real strange (because he was high). I didn't realize this until one day he said he saw a big giant squirrel in the middle of the road. Danny liked to dress nice and he thought he was a player. All the time he was dating me, he was sleeping with other women and having babies with them, but I continued to put up with it. Whenever he would call, I would run to his rescue (BIG DUMMY). He started bringing other women around in the bar while he was hanging with Ricky. I called myself "BIG DUMMY" because I did not want anyone else to call me that. When his sister would go out, he would stay home and babysit. He would meet other women and he would have them help him babysit. In the process of that, he would call me on the phone like he wasn't doing anything.

There was one young lady he started dating while he was dating me. I called to break up with him. We both got pregnant though. She had her baby in September and I had my son Jewel in October. We both had boys. I still kept messing around with him even though he was fooling around with other women until one day I just decided to leave him alone (for a little while). Now he didn't know that all the time we were talking, me and his sister had a close relationship and she would tell me when I called that he had company.

Knowing me, I would leave out of the house and there he was with another woman. I remembered his mom telling me one time that I could fight her son, just scratch him up a bit, but don't kill him. Danny had a bad temper. He would fight a woman without any problem. I remember Mary and I talking on the phone and we kept going back and forth about who could have him. She ended up leaving him alone and little ole dummy me kept messing with him and he started seeing this psycho girl.

He met this girl, and him thinking he's a player, thought he had left Mary alone but he hadn't. She was so into him that she threatened to beat up everybody. He called me on the phone and wanted me to bring him some cigarettes and I took them to him. I had told him if he had company, I was not coming over, but I did anyway. I knocked on the door and his sister said come in, she was sitting on the couch and I asked her where Danny was. She didn't say anything she just smiled and pointed to this room where he would take the other girls to. I knocked on the door to the room. Then I was banging on the door. He never came out and I gave the cigarettes to his sister and I left. I left him alone again. His sister ended up moving and I didn't know at the time the girl was pregnant by him. This baby was due in February. I found out that they were fighting a lot and she would always threaten me and Mary. She was going to kill us and our kids.

In October when I went into labor to have my baby, she had a miscarriage. He never came to the hospital while I was in labor. I was in hard labor. She kept threatening to kill our kids because she had lost hers. I asked Danny how he could allow her to threaten to kill his kids. He said, "I ain't gonna let her do nothing to y'all." I said, "I know you not, let her touch my baby and see who goes to jail!"

Danny hooked up with my brother Roscoe one time and they were getting high with some other guys. They were down at my sister Ida's house, and they were doing some drugs. Danny liked to shoot up, they called it skin poppin'. He would get drugs from my brother what they called a speedball.

They ended up having to get him out from under a car. They don't know how he got under there and they took him home to his sister's house (she had moved again). She would call me because I believe she was afraid of him. I would go and sit with her to watch him. One day I called to check on him and to see how he was doing. I was a little afraid of him too. I didn't want him to hurt me or my son. When he was on the drugs, his true colors came out as him trying to be a player. The reason why I say this is because he was so messed up off the drugs. One day I had my sister-in-law take me and my son over there and drop me off. His sister had left him in the house by himself. They kept saying he was ok, but he wasn't. My sister-in-law was still there and he went upstairs and comes down naked as a jay bird and told her she was supposed to have sex with him. I yelled at him to go put some clothes on his naked butt and she left. Well I really think his sister called me to come over and watch because he would listen to me. They were scared of him when he got high off the drugs. After a while I got tired of going over there and I quit going. One day he took off and nobody knew where he was at and then his sister called me and asked me did I know where he was at, and I said no.

Later on she found out where he was. He had been picked up by the police. I called down to the police station and asked them if they had Danny and they said yes. I asked why and they said for his safe keeping. He was picked up downtown at LaSalle. He was sitting on the floor picking with people and throwing paper everywhere, and they took him to the State Hospital. He stayed about 30 days if I'm not mistaken.

They were trying to get him off the drugs and I think they thought he had lost his mind because they had to strap him down. I was the only one who went to see him because everyone else was scared of him. While he was in the hospital, he acted so bad, they had to keep him strapped down. He even asked me if I had my knife with me (because he knew I carried a knife on me all the time).

Finally, Danny got out of the hospital and I was still talking to him. He still kept talking to other women. I kept letting Danny dog me (young and just dumb). I can go on with my story about Danny, but he was not a good father, he wasn't a good man, he was on drugs and alcohol, and that's the way I want to end it about Danny and me.

My First Love
(*Before Danny*)

Chapter 6

His name was Michael. I was in the 7th grade when we started talking. At that time, we weren't allowed to talk to boys. We had to be home before the street lights came on. I don't know why but I liked older boys. We used to go to the YMCA on Indiana after school. We would play pool, go swimming, and play basketball. Michael would be there. He was in High School. He was kind of tall, dark-skinned, and a nice looking young man. Grandma would let us sit out on the porch in the evening and I would wait for him to walk by, just so I could see him.

On Friday we would go to Teen Town where we could listen to music and dance. Michael would be there too. But a lot of girls liked Michael (he was very flirtatious). I was in a dance group with his sister, and we would practice at his house, and he would just be hanging around watching us. I remember getting into a fight one time with a girl about him, although he would like to come and spend time with me. One day at noon she was at his mom's and wanted to fight me because we were going together. His mother got on him about it because we were at his house practicing and they were picking on us. Then it was time to go back to school (it was lunchtime).

Back then, the older guys would pick young girls to talk to instead of the girls their age. After that fight I stopped being with him so much. A few years went by and then I was in High School and I ran into him. He would come over and talk. We were just friends, no more dating. When I ended up pregnant and he found out, he said to me, "You know that should have been my baby." We remained friends throughout the years. Whenever we would run into each other, we would see how each other were doing. After Michael, it was a while before I got into another relationship. I had a relationship with a guy who thought he was going to move in with me, but that was never going to happen!

Most of my relationships lasted at least three years. All others didn't last long and most of them just wanted sex. I did not, and I repeat, <u>did not</u> sleep with everybody. Some of them I would just get money from. I started getting wiser about future relationships from the experience of past relationships. A lot of guys liked me, but if I was not attracted to them, I would not talk to them. Then along came Kenneth. I met him through my cousin and her husband (it was his friend). He started coming around my house on Avondale. It started off when he would come over to visit and we would sit around and play cards, drink and listen to music. It was just a relationship, but I'm not sure what type of relationship this was. It was just strange, but I was crazy about him.

I used to hang in the bar and he would show up. When the bar closed, I went home with him and sometimes wouldn't get home until the next day. You know how you would sit around and talk to the girlfriends about your dates, we would do that (me and my friends). One night while I was at the bar, he came in and we didn't see each other, but he saw me dancing and I think he got jealous.

From that time on, we ended up not talking much and I think he was secretly talking to someone on the side. We broke it off after this. I stayed to myself for a long time afterwards, not dating anyone else. Then one day I saw him and we rode around and talked and then I ended up at his house. One time he got mad at me and said to me that I was a young girl playing and old woman's game. Then along came Hosea, we dated for a little while. He was a liar. He said he had no one but he was living with this lady, and they had two kids together.

He was a partier and a drinker but he did work. We hung out with a bunch of different couples, some of his friends and some of my friends. He would come and visit at my house and we would drink and stuff. A lot of men play games until they get caught in it. Their friends would tell what's going on in the *friend's life* because they did not want you to get hurt. He started playing games, seeing other women, and his girlfriend ended up leaving him. He then ended up talking to a friend of mine and that is something that I hate. I never dated any of my friend's ex-boyfriends. That was a no-no, never going to happen. Just like a spider, along came Jesse. I was hanging out at the bar with my girls and he came up and bought us drinks. Most of the time that I spent in the bar was mostly dancing and socializing, not just drinking. When we would leave the bar we would go to the after-hours joint and I would see Jesse there. We would just sit and talk. Me and Jesse would make plans to meet at the bar. Jesse had a woman, but I did not know that.

I found out later. We would hang out at the bar and then go to the after-hours. My brother and my play brother would be in the bar with me and he would buy them drinks too. Jesse was dating my play brother's cousin, but my play brother wouldn't tell me. We weren't dating, we would just meet up at the bar. I was still with my son, John's dad. I told John Sr. that I was not going out with him anymore because he was too jealous. I would meet Jesse at my cousin's house. One day probably New Year's Eve, we hooked up to spend New Year's together.

We started seeing each other more, and John Sr. found out about it because I wasn't spending time with him. Then John Sr. moved out. Jesse was still with his girl but they were on shaky ground. We continued to see each other. Next thing I know, his girl had found out where he had been going, and she dropped his clothes off at my house. A little while after that, I let him move in with me. That was in 1985, my son Jewel was 13 years old at the time we started dating. He was a good man and he treated my children really good. On Thursday night he would pick me up and we would go to the bar. He had a nice car and he dressed well. They called him 'Tiny' because he was a little guy. We did everything together, even with my kids. My kids were crazy about him. He would give them money. Holidays were fun because we had our families together. I got to meet his mom and stepfather. We would go to his mom's house for Thanksgiving, and she would always call me by his other girlfriend's name because she couldn't remember my name. We would always have fun when we went there or over to older sister's house.

Things were still good with us. We'd hang out and still have fun. He'd pick me up on Thursday after he got paid. He would call and say, "I'm coming to get you," and he did. This was our routine. When I gave him a 50th birthday party, I got to meet his friends. We had that party on Indiana at my friend's house because she had a big house. That was March 30, 1997. I remember when he was in his cousin's wedding and everybody thought we were married because we had been together so long. During the reception, I met his stepbrother who was older than Jesse. His name was Larry.

Everybody was saying how much of a good couple we were and asking when we were going to get married. We continued to be together and our families would get together during the holidays. Then I met some of his cousins who were partiers, but I did not really know what type of people they were. Then I met his cousin who lived around the corner from us. He and his girlfriend were okay. He talked about how ugly Jesse's other girlfriend was. Jesse was the type of guy who did not like to hurt people's feelings.

Jesse began hanging around a couple of guys from work that had the same shift as he did. Then I noticed that the regular nights we would go out started changing. I begin to start sitting at home and not worrying about going to the bar. Then his time started changing and he started hanging out later and later with his friends. I noticed that he started not picking me up to go out and one day my brother Roscoe asked me to go and hangout with him, and at first I said no, then later on I went with him anyway.

We would sit around the house and party, drink, and play cards. So one night he decided to take me out and we went to the bar and stayed until it closed, then we went to an after-hours place. He was always hanging out with this one guy named Ben. We were sitting in the car in the parking lot and he and Ben had been smoking something, I thought it was marijuana but it had a different smell to it. I told him I had to get out of the car because of the smell. Back then they called it "cocoa puffing" (which was smoking crack) on weed. Every time he would get off work, he and Ben would be together with another guy. Ben was cool but Dave was a jerk. I found out later that all three of them were cocoa puffing.

One day when it was warm, his cousins came over and he went in the kitchen and shut the door. The kids wanted to know why they couldn't go in the kitchen, and I told them that Jesse was in there with his cousin. I ended up talking to Jesse and found out that they were in the kitchen getting high smoking crack (I didn't know his cousin was strung out on crack). I had to put a stop to it. They kept coming over because they were using Jesse for a place to get high and I don't think he realized it. I had to tell him to tell his cousins to stay away from my house.

Jesse did not like it, but I told him that his cousins needed to go somewhere else to get high because I was not taking my kids freedom at home from them. Sometime later, I started noticing that things were changing and not for the better. Jesse got an attitude about it and I told him that I didn't care this was not the house to come and get high at. They did stop coming around. I didn't know that Jesse was still hanging around them. One of Jesse's cousins was getting married and Jesse was in the wedding. He was dressed real nice in his tuxedo. When we got to the reception, one of his older cousins walked up to us and asked us when we were going to get married (I looked at her and really didn't respond. We had been together about four years at this time).

Jesse's cousin told him to stop dealing with them, and gradually he stopped dealing with them. Jesse and his cousin would hang out together and play chess, and that's when Jesse said he would stop hanging around them. Jesse kind of mellowed out some from getting high, so I didn't notice much if he was still getting high. I stayed at home and took care of my kids. Family would come over sometimes. Jesse and Ben would hang out together more than anybody. Ben didn't drive so he would call Jesse and he would go and pick him up. He would go pick up his brother too. His brother would have women over for Jesse to meet when they were getting high.

After a while, I started disliking his brother because he would lie for Jesse. I would ask him where Jesse was and he would tell me he did not know. As time went on, I noticed things got worse. He started staying gone after he got paid. He started looking bad, losing weight. When his mom would have Thanksgiving dinner, Jesse would wait until the last minute to go to her house. His stepfather noticed that something was wrong. His mom still had no idea. I would tell his baby sister a lot of things like what he was not doing. Then I got me a new job and he told me not to ask him for a ride to work. He got lazy and trifling. He did not want to do anything. He would go to work just to get a paycheck. Somewhere around 1984-1985, I went into the hospital to have a D & C and I got sick behind the surgery. I was having really bad headaches and I couldn't sit up or lay down.

I was in pain every day. I did not know what was wrong. I had to go back and forth to the doctor to find out what was wrong. They ran tests and everything. I found out that I was sensitive to hot and cold. I also found out that I had fibromyalgia. It affected my right side. Jesse was no help to me he was more of a burden. My children were there to help me. My kids were getting mad at Jesse because he wouldn't help out or help pay bills. I was not supposed to get upset. Then he started blaming me for everything. I started going to a pain treatment center for my problem. I had a hard time getting him to take me to the laundry or even to the grocery store. When he stayed out all night, he only wanted to sleep until he got hungry. The whole time I was sick, I watched him hit rock bottom. One time while I was still hurting, we had a party for my sister Ida and a friend at our friend's house. I asked Jesse to come and he said no (he had been getting high). My dad and his wife were in town and they came to the party.

Jesse finally showed up at the party. Earlier that day we got into an argument. When Jesse arrived at the friend's house, he passed out at the front door. He got up and said he would be okay and he got him some air. That's when I knew things were really, really bad. Whenever we had family functions, he would participate but not too often. My dad and my brother Roscoe were my protectors. They would ask what was wrong with him. Whenever we were around my dad, he would act totally different. One time we went to Detroit in his Buick Electra 225 (it was sharp) and we partied and drank (we were at my dad's apt.). My dad took him in the room and told him that he was giving me a gun and my dad showed him another one and told him that if he touched me he was coming after him with the other one.

Jesse said we don't fight and my dad said just in case. My dad would question my son about whether or not Jesse was putting his hands on me. Even the Christmas's were starting to change. At first we would go shopping together for the kids and then he stopped caring. I ended up having to do side jobs because of my illness and that I stopped asking him for anything. He would lie around all day and do nothing and was always cold. Whenever someone would call for him, we would tell him and he would get mad. I started cussing him out (I was in counseling at the time). I would go to my cousin's on the weekend and party without him.

Whenever I would go to counseling with Cindy, I would tell her everything. When I would not talk about him, she would ask me how Jesse and I were doing. I tried sometimes not to talk about him. It got so bad that I started having a hatred for him. I just got to be so mean to him. I stopped talking to him period. Jesse got really bad. The only thing he would do was go to work. I wouldn't see him after Thursday, which was payday. That's when I knew things were really bad with the drugs. He stopped picking me up. We stopped doing everything together really. I noticed how his appearance changed.

He stopped caring about himself. He stopped taking care of himself. He started losing weight. He was already small. He had his mom and dad thinking that I wasn't doing anything for him. I talked to his sister, so she knew the real deal. Some of his family members thought the same thing until one day they came over and saw the truth. I told his stepfather and he told Jesse's mom. She started taking up for him. She did that for a little while. I guess he got tired of the relationship and stopped coming home. When he ran out of money then he would come home and get in my bed to go to sleep, and complained the whole time. I had got a job cleaning at Southwyck Mall in the morning. I told him about it and he said, "How you gonna get to work, don't ask me to take you to work!" The only time I felt he would pick me up was when I got paid and he wanted to "borrow" some money.

He always paid me back though. On the weekend I would go out with my girlfriend's and when we left the bar to come home, I wouldn't even sleep in my bed, I slept on the couch. He came to me and said to me that he remembered when he used to do that because he was out cheating with other women, so I guess now he knew how I felt. I think in his mind he decided that he was moving out and going to live with his mother. I felt a little sad but had no more tears to cry. I said 'ok.' We remained friends though. We would talk on the phone. He still wouldn't leave the drugs alone. He would call and ask me for $20 and I would tell him yeah because I knew he would give me back double. Jesse was one of two men that I really loved and I was in love with him.

He loved my kids until the drugs took him away. To this day we are still friends. After Jesse and I broke up, I stayed to myself. I wasn't trying to get into another relationship. I just wanted to be by myself and get my mind and myself together. No other man lived with me ever again. I learned my lesson. I only went out with my girlfriends. Men were always in my face telling me what they would do for me. I would cuss them out. There was this older guy that was trying to talk to me in the bar. I found out that he had a girlfriend and a wife. I asked him what did he want with me. When he would see me out, he would ask me how I was doing. I would speak and then walk away. I guess I met this other guy but right now I can't remember his name.

He was a DJ at the bar. He was there all the time. Years went by before I saw him again. Me and my friend and my sister went to this cabaret party and it ended early so we went to the bar and I saw him. We started dating. He was older than me too. I liked the older men. We did things together. He was kind of a secretive person. He showed me passionate affection when we were not in the company of other people. I would just always see him at the bar. After a year had passed, we got more acquainted with each other, trying to figure each other out. While we were dating, he met my kids.

They were all grown and he met my grandkids. He loved kids. He talked to them and played with the grandkids. When Christmas time came around, he would ask me what I wanted for Christmas and what my grandkids wanted and he would help me get it. We continued to see each other. We would run into each other in the bar. Then I started to see something in him, like a little flirtation going on with other females.

I found out that he was a church going guy. I met one of the DJ's under him (they worked for a DJ company). My sister and I would come in and sit back where they were DJ-ing. Even though he was flirtatious, I found out he had a jealous streak in him. It wouldn't show while we were out, but later after we left and went home. After the bar was over, I would go home with him and then go home on Saturday. We would talk for long periods of time. He asked me did I go to church and I said yes I did for a while and then I stopped going. He said I should try going like the first Sunday or the last Sunday. I laughed and said I would. We continued to date and then I met his mom. I didn't think she liked me. She was a quiet person.

The first time I met her, I just stayed in the car. We would go to the movies together and have fun but I was still seeing changes in him. One day I was talking to my sister and told her that I was not going to ride the merry-go-round with anyone anymore. I think we dated about four years. He would buy me gifts for my birthday, Valentine's Day and Christmas. He used to tell me that I was too young for him. Within 2 or 3 years, I started seeing changes. One was that he would say, "The woman wasn't supposed to call the man, the man is supposed to call the woman." I laughed and told him to quit trippin' and being old fashioned. After about 2 ½ years, I met one of his sisters, she was real nice. She was also married. I met her whole family. He told me how he felt about me and he ended up asking me to marry him, and told me to go and look for my ring.

My sister and I went to the mall to look at rings. I saw a couple of rings that I liked. There was one particular ring I saw that I liked. I got the prices and took them back to him. I showed him the prices of the rings that I looked at and he said, "Ooh, that's too much!" I don't know if he was joking or not. A little bit after that, I saw even more changes in him that I didn't like. He would continue to tell me that I was too young for him. I noticed that I kind of slacked going to spend the night at his house. I started pulling back away from him. This was on Friday and I had gone with him to his mom's. I was sitting in the car and he told his mom that he had asked me to marry him.

I was shocked because I didn't think he meant it. He also made a comment that my family was very overprotective of me. Some of the changes I noticed came around Christmas time. One day we went shopping to buy gifts for the kids; we were sitting at his house wrapping gifts when somebody knocked on his door. It was a lady and she started hollering at him. She was having a tantrum and she was drilling him with different questions and comments.

She told him that he said he was only going to marry her. He never commented or I didn't hear him because I was downstairs. She wanted to know how old I was. "She young" was her comment. He told her to come and ask me. She couldn't get him riled up so she came downstairs and looked at me and then walked out the door. I was ready for her to say something. It made me think was he still messing with her? He had dated her before me, but left her alone (or so I thought) and he had told me about her as well. He came downstairs all bent out of shape and I asked him what was wrong with him. He said he understood if I wanted to leave him. She (the other woman) did that to the other ladies that he had talked to before. I told him that I wasn't going anywhere. There was a new lady in town.

We continued to date for another year. I decided to start going to church. I was just going to go only on the First Sunday, but I went more than just on the First Sunday. He was asking people about me and my family. He made a comment to me that he heard me and my sisters don't play about our men. I told him that don't nobody know anything about me and my sisters. Once I started going to church more, he would come into the church and pick me up. When the Pastor would be up preaching, he would say hug your neighbor and just because I didn't get up and come to the back of the church to hug him, he got upset and said he wasn't going to come visit the church anymore.

When I was sitting in his car, the Pastor walked up to the car and said to him, "See that girl sitting in your front seat, make sure you bring her back where you got her from." I introduced him to my dad but I think my dad saw something in him that he didn't like. He was not fond of him at all. I was sitting on my porch with my uncle and he drove by the house and kept going. I told my uncle, "There he go right there." I told my uncle that I didn't know why he didn't stop. I guess he thought I was sitting on my porch with some man I was dating. He got upset about it and I called him on the phone and I kind of got smart with him.

I asked him why he didn't come back and he said because he saw the man on my porch. I told him had he turned around and came back, he would have found out that that was my uncle. He showed me that he had been riding by my house at night time because he told me he saw a Cadillac parked in front of my house. That didn't mean they were at my house. The second incident was on Valentine's Day. Somebody knocked on my door and they were on their knees serenading me (it was him).

He asked me what I was going to be doing that day and I told him that my Pastor was having a concert in Monroe, MI and he said he might go. I never heard from him at all that day. After the concert, me and some of the ladies from church stopped to get a bite to eat at the White Castle/Church's Chicken place in Monroe, MI. Three of them got out and went into the restaurant and one of them came back and said that the Pastor's wife said not to get out and I asked why.

I turned around in the car, looked out the window and saw him inside the restaurant. I told her that I had to go in and use the bathroom. As I walk in, he is standing up and he says hi to me. He was sitting in the restaurant with the 'psycho lady' that he had dealt with before, the same one that came to his house when I was there. I told him not to say anything to me. She didn't know who he was talking to. He called me a few days later to explain. I called my sister and told her about it. I also told her that if I had not been going to church like I was, I would have gone off on him. I would have hit him because that's how I felt at that moment. It was like I didn't talk to him.

That Sunday after the concert, he came by my house to apologize and to say he that he was embarrassed. He said he told his mom what happened. Later on that day he finally told me how it happened. She wanted to go to Detroit to get some chicken because it was her birthday. When she saw us, she told him she would leave him there in Monroe. I told him he had no business being with her anyway, he was supposed to have been with me after serenading me for Valentine's Day. Me and my sister were on the phone talking and I told her again that I am not about to be on a roller coaster ride with another man and that I'm about to leave him alone.

I ended up talking to him a little while longer and marriage never came up again. I quit staying at his house on the weekends because I was going to church more and learning more about the Lord and I knew staying weekends at his house wasn't right. I was praying more and I was talking to the Lord and I asked HIM to show me if this man in my life is the man that I was supposed to spend the rest of my life with. He would do nice things and I would laugh because I had already asked the Lord if he was the one. There are more things I could say but I just wanted to get some of the good things out. The third biggest incident with him was that I had been asking God if he was the one to show me, and he showed me.

I went to the doctor for some tests and I found out that from a previous surgery, my ovaries had fell and I was in a lot of pain. I had to have surgery to have them removed. After my surgery, my daughter and her husband would come over to check on me. One day they were there checking on me and he came in. They spoke to him. I was lying in my bed and they left out. He stood in my bedroom doorway and told me that he wasn't there to stay. I looked up at him and it was not good. I went off on him. The 'old' Betty popped out. I told him to get the hell out of my house and don't look back. He stood there and thought I was playing, but I wasn't playing.

I guess he thought I would get over it but I didn't. I told my sister that I meant what I said about the roller coaster ride. I went to the Women's Retreat in Michigan and had a great time. No evening service because we were tired. I was sitting on my porch because it was nice outside and he came over. He got out of his car and stood on the walkway talking to me. He was making little hints about going to the movies or the drive-in and I didn't comment on it. Then he said, "I guess I'll go see my mom." I guess he thought I was going to say that I would go with him. I told him that I wasn't going anywhere, and I didn't want anybody asking me to go anywhere because I was tired.

I wasn't calling him anymore either. I was tired of the crazy relationships that I had put myself through. God showed me that he was not the man I was supposed to be married to. I said with the kind of surgery I had, even though it was minor, how would he have treated me if it was something bigger. The other relationships that I got into were kind of like whorish relationships because they were just to get money or what I needed or wanted. I had no guidance because my mom wasn't there and I couldn't talk to my grandmother because she got killed. Some of my behavior was learned behavior because of what I saw and who did it.

I feel like all these relationships came about because of the lack of a role model and generational family curses. My mom died in 1962, so coming up with my siblings, my mom had her picks or favorites of her children (both boys and girls). Not thinking that I was not one of her favorites. I didn't know that until I got older. I didn't know if the reason she acted like that was because of her upbringing or the different relationships she was in. I can't remember a lot about my mom when I was a little girl. I can remember all the bad times but can only remember one good time and that was at Christmas time.

I can remember sitting in the front room watching TV with my siblings sometimes getting blamed for everything. I can't remember mom going to any kind of programs at school with me. I can only remember her taking me to school one time. I remember her partying with some of her cousins around her age. I can't remember any other men being in the house except my stepfather. I can remember the two of them arguing all of the time. Going outside playing, these are the things that were around me that I can remember. It's probably a lot more but I just can't remember. I remember her cooking for the holidays. I know my mom was a pretty black woman. I think I favored her somewhat.

She had the little chinky eyes. I remember how she made a difference between her children. My brother next to me was Tim. He was mistreated by our mother. I remember him being at the house on the weekend and from what I understand, my mom was married to Tim's father. He was an alcoholic and a violent person. There's not much I remember about Tim except that we always had to sit in the bedroom. I don't know why but our mother knew. Tim was raised by my stepdad's sister. They lived somewhere else.

My stepdad was not around us very much. It's not much else I can remember about Tim except how he was mistreated by our mom. The other one that was mistreated by our mom was Roscoe, my 2nd oldest brother. I don't remember a lot about the way she treated him, but one time she whooped him while he was swinging back and forth on the door. The other time was when Roscoe and I got in trouble for eating some cookies.

We didn't eat them, but the other kids did, and blamed it on us so we got punished. She made us drink syrup and water. Then my mom died and my grandmother took all 8 of us into her home. We didn't start seeing the behaviors of my grandmother until we became teenagers. Hers was more of having different men around us.

She wasn't really a drinker, sometimes during the holidays but that was it. She made a difference between us. Grandma had her picks too, and I wasn't one of them. I don't think Roscoe was a favorite either because she talked about him. My grandmother was not like my mom. I think she was whorish because of all the men she would bring around us. Her kids had different dads as well. So you can see one of the similarities that was family shared.

You could see how my grandmother caused the boys to fight over stupid stuff. It affected all of us. It made them not care a lot about each other. I didn't think my grandmother was very affectionate toward us even though she took us in and kept us together. She was the type of person who would never talk to us. She would say, "Why you want to know?" She was not a good teacher of morals. She would compare each of us against the other saying one is better than the other one. This caused us not to like each other.

My grandmother was more into her politics than with the children she was raising. She made differences between her own sisters. She talked about them too, especially the ones that drank. So of course, as kids coming up in an unstable house, we picked up bad behaviors and curses. Yes, I see it in each and every one of my siblings --- the same curses. It gets passed down through the generations, even down to our children. Even with myself, my children have different fathers.

GENERATIONAL CURSE
A CYCLE REPEATING ITSELF IN MY FAMILY

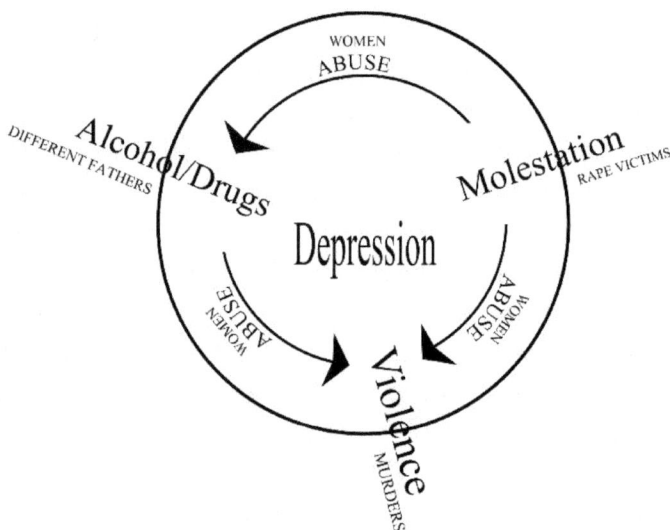

WOMEN ABUSE

DIFFERENT FATHERS — Alcohol/Drugs

Molestation — RAPE VICTIMS

Depression

WOMEN ABUSE

WOMEN ABUSE

Violence — MURDERS

As a young girl, I felt like I was shy, like I was alone, maybe a little scary as well. As I was growing up, I would let people say things to me, do things to me and I never said anything about it to anyone. Even in school I was quiet, I didn't feel like I was smart. I was scared. In grade school, I had to find something that I liked to do. It was track. That was my outlet. I remember coming up as a teenager, I would get picked on at home, but I would fight. I would defend myself. Being teenagers, I was the first niece that could go and stay at my Aunt Emma's house just to get away from home. I didn't like being at home.

With my brothers, out of the three girls, I was the one who would wrestle with them and climb trees. I was a tomboy. I would go play at the park and at the YMCA. I was always around the boys and not so much the girls. I played hopscotch and went swimming, you know, things like that. I didn't start liking boys until I was in the fourth grade. I call myself having a little boyfriend. My grandma said I couldn't have a boyfriend because I was too young. I was the teacher's pet. Back then when we were teenagers, there was a place called "teen town". My grandmother would let me go sometimes. I had my little dolls I played with, you know doing your little make believe. I would go down the street and find elderly people to talk to. Getting older, I know I started changing. No kids around, partying with my siblings. Drinking, telling our stories to each other, dealing with the different personalities (siblings). Then I started to find myself.

I had a complex about myself because of what my siblings used to say to me. So I kind of started pulling away from them. Sometimes we still went out together until I started having my own little circle of friends. I would talk to myself and say, "I'm not going to treat my kids the way I was treated." So many times I thought about running away from home. I did not trust to talk to my siblings, so I had no one to tell my feelings to. Have you ever just felt like it was just you and nobody else? I felt that sometimes when I would drink, I was numbing myself so I wouldn't feel all these things. Sometimes I wished I was with another family instead of the one I was with. I didn't have a daddy and I didn't have a mom! I would go around my friend's family, see the mom and dad, and that made me want the same. I found other people that made me feel like I was loved. Her name was Teresa. Her mom did a lot of nice things for me. It's sad that I had to go outside of my real family to find someone to love me and treat me right. I would sit at her house for hours playing with her dolls. Her mom would be in the kitchen cooking and I would stay over and have dinner with them.

My Thoughts
(Thinking About Being a Kid)

Chapter 7

You knew as a kid that you didn't talk back or ask questions why. If you did, you knew something would happen to you, by mom first or by Grandma, if she took care of you. That came from the way they were raised. Then when you got older, you wondered why they acted like that. You would never know because they would not talk to you about anything. That's what happened in my family. Secrets are not good. They will lead you down the wrong path of life. Secrets hurt you and your life so bad that you think everything you do is wrong, or not telling what happened to you and they think you are lying. So you grow up doing the same kind of things. Repeating what you've seen.

I felt like my life was upside down. Repeating what happens to you with your own family, but you know deep down inside it's not right. Watching your siblings go through the same thing and some of them would say, "We had too good of a life." I think they were in denial about a lot of what went on. But, actions speak louder than words. You get to a point where you don't want to talk about it because it hurts too bad. You just want to give up. You have no one to listen to you at all. They say, "I understand," but you know they don't.

We would sit around the table drinking, playing cards and listening to music. We were feeling good from the drinking and smoking marijuana. It was a false feeling because at that time, we'd be laughing and having fun, but full of pain. This is more of what I have felt and not telling anybody in my family. I was getting into relationships with the men that I let come into my life. I had a choice, but I made the wrong one over and over. Thinking they loved me and I loved them, I stayed in the relationship long enough to find out that they would show you their true self, whether it was good or bad. You can see how the drinking played a part in the false love. This is what comes from the drinking, being an incest victim, fighting and even death. The drinking just brings out what was already in them. This shows how their life is/was.

NO TRUST! Secrets come out when you drink! You see drug addiction and everything else. People can be so made up, but they say, "I love you, and yes you fall for it and the feeling of sex at the time." They need help too, now you see what you have been around all this time, craziness and your life will need to start somewhere, but you want it right. The word "feeling" means: an emotion, a feeling of joy and sadness; a sensation or awareness of something; a feeling of insecurity. You feel bad when you don't know how to feel, because so many things have happened to you. Do you get back at the person? Do you tell somebody or just keep your mouth shut? As you get older, life is changing for you, some of it's good and some of it's bad. I am sitting here thinking hard about this, and when I start thinking about it, it hurts and I feel like crying.

Did I do this to myself? I blamed myself for a lot of stuff that happened to me. People said they cared, but I knew they didn't. It's scary to talk about my family and how they feel about me. So you have to find someone to talk to and do they understand. You start to think life is so hard and maybe you want to kill yourself (and it seems right at the time). How many times have you thought about suicide and how you would do it? It is hard. You think of ways to get away from your family. I thought about running away or getting pregnant. Then again, not so much. It can be worse on you, running away. You can fail, get pregnant, get dogged or even get talked about not being a good mother.

You just don't want to be like your mother or grandmother or your dad, who wasn't around or in your life. It's time to change, don't do the same things that happened to them. Be better than them (my mother & father). They weren't taught the right way to be parents. That's sad and you thought the same thing about your grandmother. I love them all, but hurting so bad from the life of pain. Yes, I grew up looking at my siblings and thinking, what a life. Repeat again. Life has its ups and downs, more down than up. I got tired and wanted to get help for myself. I went to get help. I went to a psychiatrist and got a counselor.

I started talking and crying. I was hurting so bad, I got put on medication. I laughed at my cousins and friends. Watch what you say and do to others, it will come back to you. I can tell you more about my journey, but I want you to know that you can get help. We all have a story. Tell it to somebody.

Extortion

Chapter 8

Not proud of this, but having the men in my life, I learned how to play the game of money. What do I mean by that? Well, women talk to men to get money (wine & dine them), that means you sleep with them and tell them how much you care about them but deep down inside you really don't. You just want the money so you can go about your business. I did that and it comes from the life you live. I didn't sleep with all the men I talked to because I knew how to talk the game. I did it and I did it well. If people knew you did things like that, you had a name and a reputation. That game can come back and bite you hard.

LEARNED BEHAVIOR THAT CAME OUT OF MY CIRCLE

- *Partying*
- *Sex with different men*
- *Drinking*
- *Depression*
- *Drugs*
- *Getting money from men*

- o *Violence*
- o *Homosexuality*
- o *Molestation*
- o *Mental Issues*

I can say this, I know from back in the old slavery days that these kind of things happened to them, so in the blood line, it trickled down. It's the learned behaviors passed down to each generation. This is what I'm talking about, depending on who raised you, parents, grandparents or even great-grandparents, whoever. Find out what went on in your family and what kind of life did they have coming up. Once you find out what your blood line went through, you just might need help to deal with it. Don't deal with it alone.

Find out what your parents went through in their life, then you know what you need to work on. It's good to know what happened to you, then you know why you can't have good relationships with people, your children, your spouse and your family. Also that's why fathers and sons don't get along, learned behavior, passed down to the next generation. Same way with mothers and daughters. Someone should talk to you and tell you the truth so it can set you free, it will help you in the long run. God's word is true and he does not lie, He cannot lie and He will not lie.

How Change
Took Place in My Life

Chapter 9

I knew I needed help, but I had two jobs. I worked in the morning and in the evening. I felt like I was getting on my feet. I was getting off welfare and keeping food stamps. I was going to see my doctor every week or every two weeks. I went in the hospital for a D & C, but something happened and I got sick. I didn't know what was happening to me. My body was hurting and I was having headaches. The doctor didn't know what was wrong with me. I hurt so bad in my body that my children had to help me get dressed. I was in so much pain.

My doctor sent me to physical therapy. I didn't like anybody touching me because I was in so much pain. My family thought I was playing because the weekend would come and I would go out and party (I liked dancing). I didn't hurt. Eventually I found out what was wrong with me. I have Fibromyalgia. It affects the muscles in your body. I was working and feeling good about myself. I was talking to my counselor. Oh, let me say this, I had a counselor before all this happened to me. I was going for the help that I needed. I didn't like any of my counselors except for three of them. I could talk to them.

One was Sheri Page. She was my first counselor. We

had a good relationship. She would listen to me and say, "I don't understand why you are not an alcoholic or a drug addict!" I responded and told her that I had them in my family (alcoholics and drug addicts). It's all there. I loved talking to her because she encouraged me. She encouraged me to write my book years ago. I don't know what happened to her. I think she got married. It was hard for me to trust people. The next counselor I had name was Linda. We could talk for hours. She gave me time to talk. I would get to talking about what happened to me and then I would start crying. Linda always wanted to know if I was okay or did I need to go to the hospital and rest. I told her no, that I will just go home and go to my room. Linda knew a lot about me because I shared a lot with her. I could talk for a long time even though she had other clients. I felt like we had a real close bond. I wouldn't tell her everything about me and my family.

If she saw them, she could tell them their name. She could even tell some of the relationship with the men I dated. That was one part, then there was my therapy for the sex part. We talked about feelings. Did I like the men in my life and what did they mean to me? I talked about my mother, who I hated for a long time and I didn't feel good about my grandmother either. One day I went to go see Lisa, who was my new therapist. She was there to help me with my issues that I had with my family and she also was my sex therapist. She also helped me deal with the hatred that I had for my mother. She told me to write a letter to my mom and I responded, "That's stupid, she's not here to read it, she's dead!"

A week later after I wrote the letter, I saw Lisa and read the letter to her. I felt better. Lisa helped me with other stuff, like the relationships I had been in. She had me write down all the names of the men I had been with and how I felt about them. I had another appointment with Lisa and told her that I was going to write a book. She encouraged me to write my book. I found out later that she was leaving her job here and moving out of town. I told her that she was my angel. I thanked her. We talked about other things too, like about me going to find a church.

I had a doctor who I didn't care too much about because she was just there to give me medication and to see if I wanted to kill myself. You only have about 15 or 20 minutes with them and they ask you questions like, "Do you hear voices?" Then they say do you need to go to the hospital. They will drug you if you let them. When it was time to see my doctor, I didn't talk to her very much. After I would leave my doctor, I would go see Linda. Sometimes I thought Linda wouldn't ask me about Jesse but she did. I would laugh, Jesse was messed up on drugs really bad, and I put up with it. I also put up with the drinking and the verbal abuse. It went on for years with him. I thought I was going to get out of Linda's office without talking about him, but I didn't. I was in therapy with Linda for a very long time.

I cared a lot about Linda because she helped me so much. She was an angel to me. I told her about me writing a book, too. She said do it and I responded to her by saying it might be a best seller. I have had other counselors as well, two of them were men. One I didn't know and I told him that I didn't like talking to men, but I gave him a chance. The other one I didn't care about. He was always talking about the "third eye", and I felt like something was wrong with him. I didn't go back to him anymore. I went to group therapy to see how it was and it was ok.

One group was for the loss of a loved one and I talked in that group. I talked about my grandmother and how she was killed by my brother. I felt like I'd lost two people instead of one (I did lose two people). So I needed to talk around other people who had lost loved ones as well. It helped me a lot. I know I was hurting, and after a year I decided to stop drinking and smoking weed. I decided to do something different with my life, but I was still going to counseling talking to Linda about how I felt.

I told Linda that I had left Jesse alone and I also told her that I wanted to go to church. She encouraged me to do that. I didn't do it right away, but I thought about it a lot. Well, I stopped going out to the bars because I got tired of it. Seeing the same people, the same men talking about how cute you look. These are the things that I shared with Linda when I went to talk to her. I went to the bar one night and ran into an old male friend that I hadn't seen in a long time. We started talking and seeing each other. I told Linda about him. I cared about him but he had some issues. I didn't like the games he played. He had women problems. We dated for over two years. I told Linda about what I was going to do with him, I was leaving him alone. He thought I was playing but I wasn't. He talked about me going to church but I was already thinking about it. So I started looking for me a church. When we were kids, we had to go every Sunday, so I knew about church.

Dangers,
Tragedies & Distractions

Chapter 10

I was sitting in my living room watching the Gospel Channel and the Lord put this in my spirit to name one chapter of my book, "*Dangers, Tragedies and Distractions*". Danger: the possibility of suffering harm or injury; a person or thing that is likely to cause harm or injury. Tragedy: a sad event; a play in verse or prose dealing with tragic events and with an unhappy ending. Distraction: the act of distracting the mind, confusion, to distract almost to a state of madness. I talk about it in part of my book, things that happened to me in life. Dangers, tragedies and distractions can and will consume you. I talk about it throughout this book. I talk about the things that have happened to me, the dangers, the tragedies and the distractions.

Why do I call them that? It's because that's what they are and that's what happened to me in my life, and I wanted to share some more of it with you. Something I didn't want to talk about in my book was the dangers that I put my life in. The dangerous situations that I put myself in. One in particular is when we use to go to house parties and then a group of us would try to hitchhike a ride to Stickney. Me, my sister Tee, and one other guy friend of ours. This guy stopped to give us a ride but said he had to make a stop. He started saying that he knew my sister and he started talking to her.

She tapped me on my leg and whispered in my ear, and told me that he had raped her. He stopped and went into this house, and when he did we got out of his car and ran into the alley and watched the cars go by. We stopped at a friend's house nearby but as we were coming out of their house, the man we had hitchhiked a ride with came flying down the street with some other men in the car with him. He had an agenda, he was going to hurt us. We were lucky. I never tried that again. This could have been bad for all of us. Another time we were in the afterhours joint with my brother. A fight broke out and a man pulled out a gun and started shooting. I was standing right there and the bullets were flying past me. Fortunately, no one got hurt.

The first tragedy in my life was my mother and how she treated her children, bad or good. For me and two of my brothers it was bad. That led to her death. That's why we have so many distractions in our life. She must have had tragedies and distractions as well happen in her life. The second one was my grandmother's tragedies and distractions, ugly. She had men around us and they were touching us. We were picking up her bad habits like fighting, drinking, lying and treating us badly. She would talk bad about her daughter. She would say things like one was better than the other one, and so on. Then she would do the same thing with her grandchildren.

We had no father around when we were growing up. My grandmother's behavior lead to tragedy as well. We had so many distractions going on around us while we were growing up. At some point when you make your mind up to get help, go get it. You start to think you are losing your mind, yes that's what it feels like. The third tragedy is that my brother killed our grandmother. This came about because of her mistreatment of him and him being on drugs and alcohol. He never got any help when he was a kid for the things that happened to him. This is what it leads to, feeling not wanted and talked down to all the time.

The fourth tragedy is one of my other brothers used to mess with little kids. He had problems and he started smoking weed. He made wrong choices and when you make wrong choices, you end up in jail. So many things that families go through and don't want to talk about it. It comes from behaviors that were set up back in the day. Keep it silent, don't tell anybody. Don't even talk about it. You wonder why you are so jacked up. Tragedies and distractions can be bad, but go get some help so they won't repeat with you or your children.

The fifth tragedy – me, from all of the things that have happened in my life. If I had not decided to get help, where would I be right now? Where would this have taken me? I could have ended up on drugs, I could have become an alcoholic, I could have lost my mind, I could have ended up being a prostitute. I could have been killed or killed somebody and ended up in jail for life. I could not have been a good mother to my children. You don't want your tragedies and distractions to take you over. Know that you can come out of this life. I almost let it happen to me, but I had great help and I found a church. I found JESUS!

Well, I found a church home. I went to church for two Sunday's, and on the third Sunday the Pastor was preaching a message that touched my heart. I was talking to one of my sister's and she asked me if I was going to join church and I responded to her saying that I would. She has been going to

New Bethel church for a whole year and still hadn't joined. I guess she forgot how we would talk on the phone for hours about the Lord. She knew I had been going through things and she was too. When the Pastor opened the doors of the church and asked if anyone wanted to give their life to Jesus to come to the altar (I remember the dress I had on when I joined), I got up with tears in my eyes and I walked down to the altar and gave my life to Jesus. The Pastor was happy that I gave my life to Jesus. He explained to me what I had done. This was July 5, 1998. I was just crying and crying, but I knew it was time. I felt good. The church members explained to me about when we have Bible Study, which was on Monday nights, Family Enrichment night which is on Wednesdays. You know, some people aren't happy for you when you join church.

When the church doors were open, I would be at church. I went to all of the services and all of the revivals. I was not too quick to meet a lot of people though, but a sister in bible study would always take notes and make copies for me if I asked for them. She would make copies for the others as well. We became close. She would call me to see if I needed a ride to church. Sometimes I would take the ride. On the days when it was warm outside, I would walk to church because I only lived around the corner. You know people are always watching you, and family is watching you as well.

I didn't realize that my daughter was watching me because one Sunday while I was getting ready for church, I realized my daughter had gotten up and got ready to go to church with me. We went to church and she enjoyed the service. The next Sunday she was ready to go back. The following Sunday she went again. The next thing I knew, she joined church. Even though she joined, we continued to go to different services and revivals. I got a chance to meet different people, some famous and some not so famous. Being in church, I learned more about God. I learned how I was supposed to act and dress as a Christian woman.

It was more than just going to church you had to get connected with God. When the church went out of town, I would go every chance I got. When you are a babe in Christ, you are constantly learning. Someone in Bible Study told me to write down in a journal one scripture at a time until you know them. You get to know your brothers and sisters in church. Whenever they had noon day prayer I would go. I was encouraged to read my word daily. My Pastor always told us that we should not take his word but read God's word for ourselves because the word is in the bible. Sometimes Pastor would have special services and they would last a long time.

That was when I started feeling like something was going on with me and I couldn't explain it. I still didn't know a lot of people so I didn't talk to anyone about it. When I went home, my sister Ida was outside of my house with one of her friends talking and they saw me. She asked me what I had to drink, and I told them I had been to church and that I felt good. They responded, "Oh!" I just couldn't explain it. That following Monday, my Pastor was teaching bible study and he broke it down and explained to me what was going on.

It was the Holy Spirit. He encouraged me to seek the Holy Ghost and stay in my word. With me going to church like I was, I started to get to know the other brothers and sisters of the church. I learned their names and they were very nice. I would volunteer to help if help was needed. I had trust issues still so it took me a while to know my church family, even the Pastor's wife.

Finally, I got up enough nerve to meet the First Lady. She was in noon day prayer as well. I loved noon day prayer because I felt like it set the mood for the day, and she always encouraged me to pray. Even though I was going to church, I noticed how my family started acting with me. They were acting funny toward me and talking stupid. My brother Roscoe did this to me also. They stopped coming around because I wasn't doing the same things they were anymore.

Church

Chapter 11

Like I said before, I needed to learn more about Jesus. I loved going to noon day prayer. I remember being at one noon day prayer and I started speaking in tongues and I didn't know what was happening to me. My First Lady explained to me what was happening. She said we sounded like we were speaking alike in the same tongue. Another time my First Lady called me and asked me if I was ok. She wanted to know because it was hot outside. She came and picked me up and took me over to her house to cool off. She is always concerned about others. Another time some of the sisters in the church were talking about their past and I spoke up about how I used to drink and smoke. They looked at me and said, "What?!" like they were surprised.

I started helping out when we would have dinners. I would help serve the food. I liked doing things like that. I remember some of the times I couldn't go out of town because I didn't have the money for food and the hotel room. Me and my prayer partner said we were going next time. We did what it took to go. We sold dinners and pies. When the next time came around to go out of town, we went. I miss my prayer partner. We used to talk all the time and prayed together as well. We started going to bible study together. We talked about different things that we saw in church. What we liked and what we didn't like. We loved going to church.

She is one the reasons why I go. She knew I was depressed because we would talk on the phone and she would pray with me. The church started having prayer on the weekend and me and Mo would be there and have a great time in the Lord. Let me say this, I started trusting a little more. I loved to hear my Pastor preach because I always got something out of his messages. One day my daughter and I went to church and we saw this short man in the pulpit preaching. I and my daughter were talking about him, how he looks like Kirk Franklin.

She had me laughing. He is the Asst. Pastor of the church. That man can preach as well. As years went by, I learned more and more about Jesus. You see things happening around you, like people leaving the church, and then they come back. Pastor talked about this service in Memphis called the Soul Winner's Conference. I didn't get to go the first year, but I was blessed to go the next year. I wanted to go, but I didn't have enough money and some of the sisters from the church were going and one of them asked me if I still wanted to go and I told her that I still do. I don't know who the sister was that blessed me to be able to go (I think I know who it was). She has blessed me a few times.

Let me tell you about her. She can preach the word of God. She is a strong woman in the Lord. Yes, I love her. The more I learned the scriptures, the more I learned about Jesus. One of my favorite scriptures is Philippians 4:13. This scripture has helped me when I thought I couldn't do it. I have another scripture that I like as well that has helped me get through my day. I started writing a journal of scriptures and who preached them. I can't put everything down because it is so much. Yes, once you have been in church, you see a lot of things going on.

You start to look at things differently. Then you begin to think about things, people and stuff you have done. We have a women's service on Sunday, but let me back up a minute. The women of New Bethel met a very powerful woman in the Lord and she became our spiritual mother. She taught us about consecrating ourselves and what we needed to do. She also taught us about knowing the voice of God. She said that we needed to get up at 3AM and pray, write a journal, then do it again at 6AM. She taught us about what we should eat and drink during our consecration. We did this for 30 days. We became her spiritual daughters.

I tell you what, you should watch who you call your spiritual mother. She was no joke, but she helped me get closer to Jesus and helped me to hear his voice. They were talking about this other Spiritual Mother that the New Bethel women were not ready for. Guess what, we weren't ready for her. This is the first time I met Mother Dupree and oh my God, she was no joke! The women were definitely not ready for her. I remember church was going to start at 4PM and there were a few of us that were still slain in the spirit after the morning service, in which Mother Dupree had preached. We didn't know what happened. They had to get us up off the floor. We were drunk in the spirit. I have had some great experiences with the Lord. Another time, my Pastor was preaching and asked that whoever wanted the Holy Ghost to come to the altar.

I was one of the people that came to the altar and started speaking in tongues. Another time at a Wednesday night service, we went to the altar for prayer and Pastor was praying for all of us and he laid hands on us or at least I thought he did. I thought he touched me, but my sister told me that he didn't touch. It was God that touched me and I fell down. I was talking to my sister about it and we laugh because I really thought someone touched me. More years have gone by and I am yet learning more and more about my God and loving it! I know his voice and I am constantly learning how to pray.

I anoint my head before I pray and fast all because of the encouragement that came from my Pastor, First Lady, the Assistant Pastor, and Missionary Dwight. I had to talk to my Pastor about what I needed to do to become a Deaconess in the church. He encouraged me to study my word and come to the meetings. My prayer partner became a Deaconess as well. I ended up learning more about the church and I started helping one of the sisters at the church. She was the church secretary. She helped me too.

My daughter joined the Missionaries Circle. When I tell you she can preach, she can preach. I love hearing my daughter preach the word of God. Me and some of the sisters from the church started going to Mother Dupree's church. Out there, you might go in walking, but somebody was going to have to put you in your car after it was all over. Sometimes during noon day prayer, one of the Evangelist's from the church would come and open the church. We would pray and talk to the Lord. This was a time to worship and feel the presence of God. Our Pastor would let us have shut-ins at the church. We would spend the weekend with Jesus. I knew that to join any auxiliary, I would have to take an 8-week class called the New Members Class.

After we finished this class, the teacher would let the Pastor know that we completed the class and we would receive a certificate. The class was a lot of fun and we learned a lot from our teacher and she helped us a lot. She would give us homework and then the next week we would talk about it.

Whenever the First Lady had to minister in Mansfield, we would travel with her and after coming home, I would write down my thoughts and pray before I went to bed. I would get up praying and at night I would write down about my day. I would write down everything I did and everything I dreamed about as well.

We started meeting our Pastor and First Lady's acquaintances in the gospel because they would come to our church and preach or they would participate in musicals and conferences that we had at our church like the Truth Marches on Conference. One of the mothers that we got closet to started calling us her daughters. There were about 12 of us. She asked us if we want to hear from God, did we want to hear more of his voice. So she gave each of us instructions about consecration. We didn't really know a whole lot about consecration but the letter explained it all to us. We had to get up at 3AM and talk to God (we had to wash our face first and anoint our head). That was the time with God. It was in the still of the morning and you could clearly hear God talking to you.

I did it a couple of times and I was speaking in tongues again. I started learning a lot more about the Spirit of God and I started having dreams. I would tell my prayer partner about some of my dreams. I listened to different things people would say and I learned a lot about being on a consecration. God would talk to me and show me things. I remember telling a couple of people that God was working on me fast and it scared me because I didn't know why. I had to pray more and talk to God. I started getting around more of the sisters in the church. I started calling them 'sis' and we would talk and go to bible study and church services together. When I started going to church, I only had the clothes I went out to the club in. I was taught to be a lady and wear a dress to church.

That's the way we had to dress for church. I got a few

more and my First Lady blessed me as well. Some of the ladies went to Detroit shopping with her. She helped me a lot. Showing me and helping me to look good. I knew how to dress but she showed me another way to dress and I liked it. I thanked her for helping me. I knew that God was blessing me a lot because we had services where nobody could move. People were laid out in the spirit. Pastor Allen would have shut-in service on Good Friday and we would spend the night with Jesus praying, singing and laying out before him at the altar. Pastor would also hold a conference every year called the Truth Marches on Conference, and people would come from all over the United States to be at this conference. He always had special guests that either ministered or sang at his conference. They were famous well-known people in the world of Gospel music. The church doors would open at 6PM and service would be over at 11PM sometimes.

Pastor would bring the best singers and great pastors to minister to God's people. He had this conference every year and it was a free conference. My pastor also travels a lot with his group "The Rance Allen Group", because he is a famous world renowned Gospel singer and Evangelist. Whenever he is away from his home church I miss him. I would always pray for him to return home safely. He calls us his babies and he always try to get back home to his church family so he can continue to feed us God's word. He would never leave us without anyone who could minister to us while he was away. He has a very capable ministerial staff which includes the Assistant Pastor, the First Lady and his brother. He has a great choir as well and they can sing very well. We also have a band that he calls the Church House Band", and they are really, really good.

Let me tell you about the Assistant Pastor, Elder Dupree. I know my Pastor trusts him because he acts just like the Pastor. I told him that one time. When he preached, it was like hearing our Pastor preach. Whenever Pastor would get up to preach, he would talk about his Assistant Pastor being single. I always wondered why he did this. I never asked. Let me say this, people watch you in church and they start thinking they know things, then they start coming and talking about the Assistant Pastor being single and saying stuff like, "He single, you single." I didn't think anything about it and I wasn't thinking about him like that either. I wasn't in church trying to get a man, my focus was learning about God. I remember talking to one of the sisters that I know in the church and told her what somebody said to me about the Assistant Pastor and she said, "What's wrong with it?" I said no, at the time I wasn't talking to anyone and I was getting ready to leave my ex alone.

One day my daughter and some of the younger ladies were talking about the Asst. Pastor had a son but they had never seen him. We saw the daughter and the youngest sons, but never the older son. So one day he came to church and the young ladies were saying that he was the Asst. Pastor's oldest son. They found out his name. My daughter told me that he was the Assistant Pastor's son. One day I saw him with my daughter talking to her and I got a chance to meet him. He's a nice young man. I told the Elder that I had met his older son.

Then I saw him at my house and I put two and two together and realized that the Assistant Pastor's son and my daughter were seeing each other. I just watched and didn't say anything. My daughter joined the choir. I told my daughter that I was going to be baptized again. I took the dip and my daughter and grandson got baptized after me. My daughter was preaching at other churches with the missionaries doing the Flames of Fire. I call her my Paula White.

She doesn't use notes. God gave her the spirit of

preaching. Then on some Sundays after church, some of the saints would go out to eat with the Pastor and his wife, and others. Sometimes I would go. The Elder and I would talk but that was all. Then it came time to go to Memphis for the Holy Convocation. He told me that he takes his mom and dad with him when he goes. It was his gift to them. One time I said to him to put me in the trunk and take me to Memphis, he started laughing.

They went and came back safely. I saw him sitting back in the pulpit. Sometimes I would be looking at him and my sister would tap me and say he's looking at you. I would tell her "No he isn't." I would call him sometime but not a lot. I knew he was a busy man. I told him that was good. One day we were talking on the phone and I needed to ask him something. I needed some help with something. He talked to me and it helped. We noticed that people were trying to see what was going on between us, but nothing was.

We would just talk on the phone. We started talking more and more. I wanted to take him to dinner but I was scared to ask him because I thought he had a lady friend. So one night I was talking to him on the phone and he said he wanted to take me to dinner for my birthday and I said yes. He came and got me, we had dinner, we talked and then he brought me home. We started doing things together. Nobody knew but one person. I told him I would like to go to Memphis with him and his parents. I wanted to go this time but I needed to get some money. So I sold dinners and he helped.

I made enough money to go with him to Memphis. Other things started happening in our life. I felt that I could invite him to dinner and I did. We started spending time with each other and having fun. A lot of people in the church didn't need to know about me and Elder, and some of my family was asking about us. What I do know is that our relationship didn't have anything to do with anybody else. People were trying so hard to find out. We heard the things that were being said about us. Good. But as long as God knows, that's all that mattered to us. So in Memphis, Elder told Pastor Allen about us. Yes, we are a couple and the only thing I can say was, "GOD DID IT!" and I thanked him.

Now I can close this chapter of my life. Yes, this has been a hard and learning way. But God has released a lot of pain and hurt out of my life and now my new life has begun. I have noticed that God is doing something new in me and it feels really good!

Letter
To My Children

I have three beautiful children and I know they love their mother. They watched me go through my crazy life and they knew it was always not good. We got through all the bad problems we had, but I know that they can say that I was a good mother to them. Everything wasn't always great though. We had some hard times but we made it. I took care of my children. I made sure they had clean clothes, even if I had to wash them out by hand. I fed them well, and they didn't miss any meals or snacks. Most of all, I didn't let my children be with just anybody.

I was very protective of my children and they did not get everything they wanted. I gave them birthday parties and checked on them in school. I was very involved in their schooling. I didn't believe in letting them hang around the grown-ups, especially when we were partying because there was drinking and smoking going on. I told them that each one of them has a brain and each one of them was different from the other one. I taught them to respect others and respect themselves as well. I taught them to do the right things. I didn't share a lot of my past with them because they didn't have anything to do with it. I did not want to put them in my mess.

I knew one day that they would have their own families

and I didn't want my mess to influence their lives in any way. I watched my children grow up to be good children, but now I see my children going through some of the same things I did, and I don't want that for them. I wanted better for them. My children are good kids and they are not messy. I watch them constantly. I just want them to live right and enjoy their life. I thank all of my children for all of their love, care and support that they have given me down through the years. Even in my sickest hours, they were there for me, they helped me when I couldn't help myself and I thank them for that. Thank you for everything you have done for me, and know that I love you very much, and God bless you.

Now you have your own families, take care of them and love them unconditionally. Do the right thing by them and the right things to take care of them. Family is important. You are very smart and funny. Continue to love your aunts, uncles, and the rest of your family. To my children, this book is very important to me. I've waited a long time for this book to happen, and again, I love all of you very much.

For My Grandsons

＊━━◇◆◇━━＊ ∿⊘⊘⊘∿ ＊━━◇◆◇━━＊

To all of my grandsons, I want you to know that I LOVE YOU! To the ones I help raise, know that I love you because you were there with me while your mother was working. I kept an eye on you all even though I had some issues. Now watching you grow up has been a joy. I have talked to you about life and what you want to do in life. Do better than me. Finish school, get a good job and own your home. Life has changed me. Go to church and keep Jesus Christ in your life. Just a little thought, plan for your life.

And I would like to give a special thanks to Deshawn for helping his granny with the idea and concept of the front cover.

For My Dad

In my book I say some things about my dad but I have more to say to him. Dad, you came into my life when I had my first child. I didn't know you but I heard a lot about you and they were not very good things. I heard that you were in the army and that they were looking for you, but you were nowhere to be found. I know you knew you had children but it was like you didn't care. One time on the radio, a cousin of yours said your name and you responded to him, and that's when we found each other again. It was a long time, but it happened. It wasn't nice when I met you and my other brothers and sisters. You lived the street life so hard that you didn't know how to talk to your children. Living a life in the streets is very hard. I heard that you were a player and had a lot of women, so you thought it was okay to talk to us with no respect. Then when you came around again, you were high, talking crazy, and I had had enough, so I told you off. I got respect from you after that. You would talk crazy to everybody else but not me. You just didn't care, but that was your lifestyle.

You kept coming around to see us. We began to get close and we talked a lot. I came to visit you in Detroit and stayed with you and your wife. I don't know why, but you didn't trust her. I can't tell everything about you Dad, I just know that we became very close. You shared things with me about my mom and why y'all didn't make it. I found out that you loved her but people got in the way and you left. I came when you got married again (you kept getting married). Your wife was a nice lady, and we were around with you and her. I don't know what happened, but you didn't want to stay married to her. You had to have surgery and I came to stay with you for a couple of days. After the surgery things didn't get better because then you called me and told me that you were moving to Toledo.

We talked about why you and mom didn't make it. We became even closer and I forgave you. You told me you were sorry for not being in my life. I said I'm grown now but we can take it from here. We talked and did things together. You spent time with all your grandkids but you were closest to my oldest son. You would call my daughter granddaughter because you couldn't remember her name. You had a problem with drinking and smoking for a long time. You lived a fast life but it was rough for you. You told me you were put out at the age of 12. I knew you weren't well because you told me that and I didn't want to hear it. You told me where things were in case something happened. You told me that you and your sister didn't get along. We started doing more things together as time went on. You did tell me that you didn't like the man that I was talking to because you knew he wasn't right. You saw it for yourself. You didn't want anybody messing with your children or grandchildren. You said you would kill somebody about us. You were very protective of us. I am so grateful that I had the chance to be with you Dad. I know you had a problem with us drinking and getting high after a while because of what you went through. I know that you didn't really like seeing my brother high because he didn't know how to act. He acted crazy just like you did.

One day you told me to stop drinking and I told you that I didn't drink anymore and you said, "Good." I know you had secrets that you didn't tell anybody about, but because we had gotten close, you would talk to me. To this day, nobody knows what we talked about. I know why you acted the way you did and why you wanted to protect us. Your life was very, very crazy. When you were getting very sick, you told me but I didn't want to hear it, but I started listening to you. I'm going to stop talking about my dad because I miss him very much. I ended up loving him even when I was mad at him. I love you Dad.

To The Other
People in My Life That I Love

Let me say this about the other people in me and my children's life. I like meeting good people. We met these two people that came from down south. It was in the summer of 1972 after I had my first son. I would walk to the store and this old lady would speak to me and I wouldn't say anything to her. She had a daughter and she would say hi to me every time she saw me and I wouldn't say anything back. The next time me and my son walked to the store, they saw us and spoke to us and this time I spoke back. We began to get close with each other. I let them meet my children and they love my kids. The old lady started watching my children while I went to school and worked. We called her Mama Joe. My children loved her and her mother. I didn't have to worry about my children eating or anybody touching them. I trusted Mama Joe and her mother. If they messed up in school, I would send them to Mama Joe and she would get them back on track in school. I didn't talk to everybody because I didn't and wouldn't trust people. Well, I moved to Woodland Ave. and lived there for 5 years. I went to the block meetings, but I didn't talk a lot at those meetings.

There was this lady named Mary who took to me, and I told her that I didn't trust people. She told me that I would have to trust people one day. I saw her a week later when she stopped in front of my house and talked to me. She wanted me to go take a ride with her. We became very, very close, and I started calling her mom. She let me wash my clothes at her house. She even gave me keys to her house. She trusted me in her home. She loved my children and my grandchildren. She talked to me about different things in her life. Mom did a lot for me and my children. She helped me when my gas was going to get cut off. I helped her in return. I loved her very much.

My Uncle Ward

Things have action, but I want to tell you thank you for listening to me. I have always loved my uncle ever since I was a little girl. You may not know this but I respected my uncle. Thank you for watching over me and thank you for your prayers. I didn't know that you prayed for all your nieces and nephews. I didn't know you prayed for me all that time. I just want you to know that I have a great respect for you. Uncle Ward, I pray for you all the time. I feel that I have done something right in my life that's been a long time coming, and I hope you enjoy reading my book.

To My Cousins

To my cousins (you know who you are), thank you for the love you have shown to me and my children down through the years. When I didn't have help, you helped me. I am very grateful to you. We have done a lot of things together, some of them good and some bad, but you have been there through it all. Never forget the love that I have for you.

To My Best Friend

We have been there for each other. I met you when were 19, and we had some rough times. I know we fell out with each other one time, but we got it together afterwards. I have said this to you before, if you ever need me, I am there for you. You are my little sis. We have had good times and some bad times, but we are here for each other. We have shared some secrets that nobody knows about but us. I just want to say, I love you sis, and thank you for being there. Thank you for our talks and tears. Hope you enjoy my book.

First, I want to thank my brother for bringing us together. Once we began our friendship, we were able to talk about things in my life and your life that has helped me tremendously. The things we talked about were things we didn't like. We began to get close. We could go out together and have fun. I shared with you some of the things that was going on with me and you would listen. One day I came down to talk to you and when I started talking to you, I started crying. You looked at me and asked me if I was going to be okay. I said yes. You let me pour out to you. I thank you Big Sis (that's what I called you). You told me to stop crying. I did and I felt better. But it's great when you call and find somebody you can share what's going on in your life with. You told me not to do anything more. After that, we laughed and you called me a cream puff. So again, I want to say thank you Big Sis (K).

Little Sister

When I moved on Woodland, I met a mother and daughter that lived together. The daughter had two daughters, one was 4 years old and I don't remember how old the other on was, but she was sick. This young mother took care of her two girls. Going to the hospital with one and sending the other one to school, and holding a job. She ended up losing the one daughter but God blessed her with another one. I knew it was hard on her losing her daughter. She was a very strong woman, still working and taking care of her family. We became close friends and I love her, her mother and her girls. I found a job and she would take me to work at 6AM in the morning. She didn't have to but she did. So I need to tell you how much I appreciate you for getting up so early and taking me to work.

You and your mother did other things for me and my children. I call her my little sister. I saw you put your children through school and they are great children. They even got good jobs. I told you that you deserve to be blessed. I have watched you down through the years and I love the woman that you are. I have seen your tears and we have talked. I would tell you that you are going to be all right, and you are. Now you are married and I know that's what you wanted. With all of this, I want you to know I love you, your mother, and your daughters. I have watched them grow up to be good women. You taught them very well my little sister (Star).

Godfather to My Oldest Son

This person I want to talk about has known me ever since I was a teenager and going to the YMCA. We had a place to play, swim, run, and have gym. He was one of the coaches. He talked to all of the children there. Years passed by the time I saw him again. I told him that I had gotten pregnant and he talked to me. He asked me a question, did I have a godfather for my baby and I said "no." He told me that he would be my son's godfather and that if I ever needed anything to let him know. But let me tell you this about my son's godfather, he was there for me and my baby. This man did just what he said he would do for my child. I am so grateful to him. He did more for my son than his own father did. My son's godfather didn't miss a birthday, Christmas, or school. He would call me before school started and buy his clothes for him.

If I needed anything, he was there. When my son started High School, I didn't have to check on him because he had a man in his life that cared. A great man and he stayed in my son's life. I didn't worry about him in school because his godfather talked to all of his teachers. He told my son that when he turned 18, he was on his own. But that wasn't so. He was still there for him. My son has respect for his godfather. My son started doing things he shouldn't have been doing, and one day his godfather called me and asked me if my son was alright. I said yes. He came over to check on him. So I just wanted to tell him thank you for being there for my son and me. Thank you for everything you have done for us. I appreciate you because you were there.

Why?

If my mother was still alive, I would ask her could we talk. I would ask her what happened to her when she was young. I would ask her, "Why did you treat me the way you did? Why did you play favorites? Why were you so mean? Did your mother treat you liked that?" I just want some clarity as to why you were that way with some of your children. But I saw it with my grandma, too. What happened in her life? Learned behavior. What did she have to endure in her life back in the days of slavery? Her mother had to put up with a lot back in slavery time. We just don't know. So, I called one person to see if he knew anything about my great-grandmother. My uncle didn't know. He said his mother never talked about her mother. I told him that he was right that she didn't talk about her mother. She didn't even have pictures. My grandmother didn't believe in sharing things with you.

Special Thanks

I want to give a special thanks to Sis. Shields. I appreciate you for listening to me and being there through my tears. You have been a great help to me. I thank you for all the long talks we have shared down through the years. It's great when you can trust a person and I found that in you. So I just want to say I love you Sis. I ask God to bless you and your family richly. Thank you for the laughs and being there for me. It's been a long time.

So, . . .
Let's Talk Family

Talk about the words forgive, forgiveness and forgiving. Why do we hold on to the opposite of these words, un-forgiveness and unforgiving? I know we do it and it's not good for my life or your life. I encourage my family to read it in the dictionary and see which one they are holding on to, or if you holding on to all of them. You will not be able to go forward and really enjoy life until you figure this out. You will feel like you are living but you are not. I am just asking you to stop this. We carry it for years and years, and don't do anything about it. Holding grudges in this family and then passing them down to our children. I don't have to say what it is, but each one of us do. If you want your life to get better, do something about it. Yes, we all have been hurt or we have hurt someone.

So why not start now. Today, as I am writing this to my family and thinking about this, tears came to my eyes. I want to say I love all of you very much, but it is time to stop. I know it's just not our family, but families around the world. God forgave us and Jesus died for all of us. Read these scriptures on forgiveness – Psalms 86:5, Matthew 6:14 & 15, and Colossians 3:13. So why can't you forgive? Your life can and will be better. Yes, I am talking about everything that went on in this family.

We all know what I'm talking about. The good, bad, and the ugly. So let's not be like our parents and grandparents, holding on to unforgiveness. Let me say this, I forgive everyone and everything that's happened to me and I have accepted Jesus into my life, and I feel you. I talk to different ones that I had to apologize to. I felt good. God has blessed me and is still blessing me.

I was just lying here thinking we all have done some things we are ashamed of. Once upon a time in our life growing up, we had done things that we felt like we couldn't tell anybody, but right there you just can't keep living in what you have done, and don't let people hold it over your head. That's another thing you need to do and that is to forgive yourself. Forgiveness is not for the person that did something to you or hurt you, forgiveness is for you. Another thing about unforgiveness or forgiveness, is that I see people around me that are talking to me, and I think the reason why they do have problems in their relationships are because something happened to them. Somebody might have raped or molested them and they don't know how to let go. That's why we have so many problems being in a relationship. Deep down inside you're thinking about what happened to you and are carrying it every day with you, and you never went to get any help.

So what I'm saying as far as a relationship with unforgiveness, is to go talk to the person. Even if you don't want to talk to that person, get it off your chest. Write it down on paper to the person that did it to you or said the wrong thing to you, or the one that just won't talk to you. I learned while I was in counseling that if you don't want to confront the person, write it down in a letter that helps. I didn't think it was going to help me at first but it did. What I'm saying is even if that person or persons never forgive, God wants you to forgive yourself so you can get on with your life. You did what God told you to do, you asked for forgiveness and that was your biggest step, so move on and keep on going so you know that you are on the right track.

It's about 6:24AM and I am lying in bed, and I'm hearing something else about forgiveness.

About My
Aunts and Uncles

This would go with my mom, grandmother, and great-grandmother. I was really trying to put this together about my bloodline. Well, my grandmother had three brothers, but I only met two, my Uncle Johnnie and Uncle Chuck. She had six sisters and I met five of them. Back in the 1960's, one of my grandma's sisters lived across from us in an apartment building on Monroe Street. That's when grandma took us in to raise us. I don't remember her still living there. We started seeing more when we lived in the other houses. I don't remember a lot about my aunts when we lived in the other houses. When we lived on Vance St, we got to see more of Aunt Emma than any of the other aunts. When we moved on to Avondale, we saw Aunt Emma a whole lot more. My Aunt Emma was the baby girl. She was a short lady but a lot of fun to be with. She was a drinker. She liked her wine and she would dance with us. We would pick with Aunt Emma.

I remember Aunt Emma would talk baby talk around us. I noticed that when Aunt Emma would say hi to Grandma she wouldn't respond back. She would go to her room and leave Aunt Emma with us. We just had a lot of fun with her. One day, Aunt Emma came over and stayed for a while and then asked grandma to take her home. Sometimes Grandma would take her home and sometimes she wouldn't. I noticed she talked about her being a drunk and dogged her. I didn't like it. She was there for us. The next one I want to talk about is my Aunt Mary. She had a problem with people saying her name right or spelling it. Aunt Mary had a good job and she was a sharp dresser. She wore all kinds of wigs and looked good in them, but she had some problems to, she talked about what she had but she was a drinker and had a lot of men in her life.

She would treat some of her sisters bad and I think she had her picks. She would come to Toledo, pick up her sister and they would get into it. She would put her out of her car on the highway. I'm talking about things I remember. My Aunt Mary would come and get us during spring break or summer break for a week and take us to Detroit. We would have so much fun. But I started seeing different things about my aunt that I didn't like about her. She would get around other people and talk about us and I didn't like that.

So, I stopped going to Detroit for summer break. My next aunt I want to talk about is Aunt Naomi and my Uncle Charley. Aunt Naomi was a Christian lady and Uncle Charley was a Reverend. I love both of them. My auntie was a loving person and I would go over to their house. She had a nice home and a beautiful yard full of flowers. I started liking flowers too. I remember sometimes she would have her family over listening to music and partying. I would go to church with them. Aunt Naomi and Uncle Charley would come over a lot to see Grandma and us.

I don't remember a lot about my Uncle Johnny and Chuck. I knew Uncle Johnny was a short man and a drinker as well. We didn't see him a lot but he would come over and he was nice to us. Uncle Chuck was kind of mean to me, and a drinker. I don't know a lot about him but all of them would come over to our house. I think they had a rough life and I saw it as I got older.

Dedication

This book is dedicated to my Mom Annette Allen, my Dad Emanuel Justice Brown, my grandmother Mamie Lou Williams, and my brother Stanford Brown.

A special thanks to my brother-in-law Everett Dupree for the time and help that he gave in the developing and making of this book.

Special Dedication

To two special people in my life, Dad Dupree and Mom Dupree, thank you for sharing your wisdom and knowledge with me.